Hamlyn Practical Gardening Guides

GARDENING
MONTH-BY-MONTH

Peter Blackburne-Maze

HAMLYN

Published in 1989 by
The Hamlyn Publishing Group Limited
a division of the Octopus Publishing Group
Michelin House
81 Fulham Road
London SW3 6RB

ISBN 0 600 56478 9

Typeset by MS Filmsetting Limited, Frome, Somerset
Printed in Italy

GARDENING
MONTH-BY-MONTH

CONTENTS

INTRODUCTION

Although the calendar year starts in January, that, in fact, is one of the slackest times in the garden. Nine years out of ten the ground is too wet and cold to do any gardening outdoors, while in the greenhouse there just is not enough light for plants to grow properly. However, starting a gardening calendar in January does give you time to build up slowly to a fever of activity in the spring.

But first, a few words of explanation about the organization of this book. By concentrating in one chapter all the information on activities that have to be carried out during a single month there's no danger that you'll neglect any task. This arrangement also has the advantage of letting you see in advance exactly what needs to be done. You can therefore plan ahead at leisure, purchasing seeds and equipment in good time.

Each month features a selection of decorative plants that will be at their best. Although there is only space to list a few of the many possibilities, a range of de-ciduous and evergreen shrubs, small trees and climbers that have particular interest by way of their flowers, fruit, foliage or coloured stems are listed, together with some flowering bulbs and herbaceous perennials also appropriate to the month.

Many of these are illustrated as, after all, it is the ornamental plants that give the seasonal feel to a garden. By choosing a few from each section for each month you will be able to have decorative interest throughout the year – even in midwinter. Local climatic conditions and the weather will have their effect on flowering times and you may find that in your garden the *Plants for May* are in fact in flower in April or even in June!

The different climates experienced in the British Isles are always a problem when drawing up a calendar of garden plants and routine jobs. For example, Scotland is frequently a month behind the south coast of England in the spring whereas autumn can come anything up to a month earlier. Also, anyone planning what to do will have to remember that there are early years and late years. Tie this in with the state of the weather and the soil on the day that you would like to garden and you will soon realize that gardening possibly demands a greater flexibility of mind than any other pastime.

A word also must be said about varieties of plants, especially vegetables. Most varieties are notoriously fickle; what may be in vogue or considered the best when a book is written, may not be so even a year later. New and better varieties are always coming along to displace existing ones. For that reason, few varietal names are given but those that are have the merit of having stood the test of time. In the case of the vegetables, most will be found in the list of garden varieties recommended by the National Institute of Agricultural Botany (NIAB) at Cambridge.

Local knowledge as regards climate and soil, as well as local preferences as to varieties, can be a great help but do make sure that the information is reliable.

Right: Roses in high summer. 'Cerise Bouquet' is one of the modern shrub roses that needs little in the way of regular pruning and flourishes in most soils. Bush roses, on the other hand, are greedy feeders.

Opposite: In frosty weather little can be done in the garden. The ground is too hard to dig or plant and the lawn should not be walked on.

JANUARY

Although this is a comparatively quiet time of the year, don't waste a moment. Take advantage of the general lull to catch up on a wide range of activities.

FLOWERS AND SHRUBS

Planning the flower garden should be done without delay so that seeds can be purchased early. The benefits of buying early are that you will get exactly what you want, without substitutes, and that you can see the full range available before you make your choice. Half-hardy annuals (HHA), hardy annuals (HA), hardy biennials (HB) – wallflowers, forget-me-nots, etc, that will be sown this spring for flowering 12 months on, and hardy perennials (HP) – also for flowering in future years – should all be considered.

PLANTING SHRUBS AND TREES

On the active side, we are right in the middle of the dormant season when bare-rooted deciduous trees and shrubs can be planted. These are the ones that are not already growing in containers, but which have been dug up straight from nursery rows. Container-grown plants can be planted at any time of the year, provided

Fragrant flowers of witch hazel (*Hamamelis mollis*) display dainty strap-like petals during the months of winter. It grows to about 1·2 m (6 ft) and so is ideal for a small garden.

that the ground is in an easily cultivated state, not frozen or sodden.

If bare-rooted material or root-wrapped plants arrive when either the weather and/or the poor soil condition make it impossible to plant, dig out a trench, stand the plants in it, replace the soil, and tread it down firmly over the roots. This is called 'heeling in'. The plants can remain there for the rest of the winter, if need be. In

extremely bad conditions, keep the plants in a shed or garage, still wrapped up, until conditions improve.

CONSTRUCTION WORK

This is best carried out now, while the soil is workable and all the plants are dormant. This may involve building or knocking down old sheds, putting up a fence, laying a terrace, or making a rock garden.

PLANTS FOR JANUARY

Deciduous trees and shrubs

Chimonanthus praecox (winter-sweet)
Cornus alba 'Elegantissima' and 'Sibirica'
Cornus stolonifera 'Flaviramea'
Corylus avellana
Daphne mezereum
Hamamelis (witch hazel)
Lonicera fragrantissima
Lonicera purpusii

Prunus subhirtella 'Autumnalis'
Rubus cockburnianus
Salix alba 'Chermesina'
Viburnum × bodnantense
Viburnum farreri
Viburnum tinus

Evergreen trees and shrubs
As well as the many conifers and the evergreens with variegated foliage, the following are in flower:

Azara
Daphne laureola
Daphne odora
Erica herbacea (E. carnea) (many cultivars)
Garrya elliptica (catkins)
Mahonia
Rhododendron mucronulatum
Sarcococca
Viburnum tinus

Climbers
Clematis cirrhosa

Jasminum nudiflorum

Bulbs
Crocus
Cyclamen coum
Eranthis (winter aconite)
Galanthus (snowdrop)

Herbaceous perennials
Helleborus (hellebores, including Christmas Rose)
Iris unguicularis (I. stylosa)
Winter-flowering pansies

ERECTING A WINDBREAK

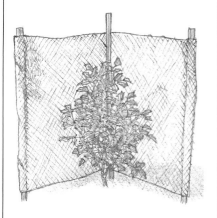

Fine gauge netting stretched round sturdy stakes gives protection to evergreens and conifers from the worst effects of cold. Young plants, especially, are susceptible to chilling winds.

DIG SWEET PEA TRENCHES

This is normally only done when they are being grown for exhibition, but it can also make all the difference when the soil is heavy clay.

You should dig the strip of ground to two spits depth, incorporating garden compost or manure into each. Ideally, the trench should be 30–45 cm (12–18 in) wide, and dug to 60 cm (2 ft) deep.

WINTER PROTECTION

If any trees or shrubs are showing signs of suffering from either the cold or severe winds, you must protect them.

When conifers and evergreens are damaged by the cold their foliage goes brown. In addition, strong winds can rock or even blow them over. This is prevented by providing trees with a stake but to avoid damaging the roots drive it in at an angle, with the top pointing into the prevailing wind. Shrubs are best protected by surrounding them with a Netlon-type windbreak; this is also good protection against cold winds.

Any heavy snow that falls on trees and shrubs, especially evergreens and conifers, should be shaken off if it starts to pull branches out of shape or even break them. However, light snowfalls are best left on all plants because the snow will act as a blanket against the cold.

Above: The weight of heavy snow can break the branches of conifers and evergreens. Shake off gently after the first fall.

Right: Snowdrops (*Galanthus nivalis*) are always a welcome sight in January. Bulbs should be divided or transplanted after flowering is over.

9

Jasminum nudiflorum looks best tied to a support or trellis rather than left to sprawl. It flowers throughout the winter months and is easy to grow.

BULBS, TUBERS AND CORMS

When bulbs which were planted in bowls (see September) for flowering indoors have 2–3 cm (1 in) of shoot showing above the bulb fibre, they can be brought indoors. First put them in a little-used and cool room until they start growing more vigorously. Never hurry them by keeping them in too warm a room or they will simply produce a lot of leaf and poor quality flowers.

Look at all dahlia tubers and gladiolus corms that you stored away for the winter, and remove any that are going rotten. If you suspect that this is due to excessive cold, provide better protection for the others by covering them with more dry peat or straw. With dahlias, you will normally be able to cut off just the damaged tubers.

LAWNS

The main winter job is to ensure that leaves and other debris do not remain on the lawn. Brushing them off will also remove any worm casts, thereby reducing the risk of weeds and moss invading and gaining a foothold.

Further damage can be caused by walking on the lawn when it is frosty. This will crush the blades of grass, and result in them going dark for the next few weeks. Some of the grass may even be killed back. You can always spot a lawn that has been walked on when frosty – it has dark green footmarks all over it.

POOR DRAINAGE

Note where any water lies after heavy rain or when snow is thawing. Drainage can normally be improved by spiking the waterlogged areas with a handfork after the winter, and by building up the depressions with several light applications (up to $\frac{1}{2}$ kg per m²/1 lb per sq yd at a time) of sifted soil at intervals during the growing season.

CHECK EQUIPMENT

Make sure that mowers, mechanical edgers, strimmers, etc, are in good working order. If any need repairing or sharpening, have them seen to by a professional. If you see to them yourself you can do more harm than good.

VEGETABLES

In a well organized vegetable garden, there should be very few empty spaces during the winter. This is the time of year when vegetables are at their most expensive and when the greatest savings can be made by growing your own.

VEGETABLES IN SEASON

Brussels sprouts, spinach beet, cabbages, and savoys, and if frost permits there will also be celery, leeks, and parsnips. Remember to check those you stored in the atumn – carrots, onions and shallots, swedes and turnips, potatoes and Dutch white cabbage – because they can easily become infested with greenfly. Full details of how to store various vegetables appear in **October, vegetables**.

PLANNING

Draw up two plans, one to list the vegetables you wish to grow, when they should be sown and/or planted, and when they will mature. The second plan is a map of the vegetable plot showing where you will plant them.

This is not quite as easy as it sounds because 'crop rotation' always has to be considered. This is ensuring that you do not grow the same type of vegetable on the same piece of land two and more years running. The reason is that this prevents a possible build-up in the soil of diseases which attack a particular group of vegetables. The chart on the right shows the different groups of vegetables and how they should be rotated. With the planning stage out of the way, all seeds should be bought as early as possible.

PREPARING THE LAND

Digging over the vegetable plot is vital. If you are gardening on heavy soil, finish digging as soon as you can. This will give the soil time to be broken up by the weather so that it can be cultivated easily in the spring. A full description of digging is found in **November, vegetables.**

If the land has not been limed for some years, or if the soil is naturally acidic, ground limestone or chalk should be applied after digging. This will be washed in

THREE-YEAR CROP ROTATION PLAN			
	Group 1 Brassicas	Group 2 Roots	Group 3 Others
1st year	Brussels sprouts Cabbage Cauliflower Kale Savoy Sprouting broccoli Kohl rabi Radish Swede Turnip	Beetroot Carrot Chicory Parsnip Potato	Peas Beans Celery Onions Leeks Lettuce Peppers Spinach Sweet corn Tomatoes Marrows
2nd year	Group 3	Group 1	Group 2
3rd year	Group 2	Group 3	Group 1

Hardy Brussels sprouts are there for the picking during winter. Just collect as many as you need for a serving. Tall kinds will need staking in exposed areas.

by the rain and will penetrate deeply into the soil. Lime helps plants to make the best use of the available nutrients in the ground. It also reduces acidity and will help to break up clay. However, if manure has just been dug in, leave the liming for one month or the lime/chalk will react with it, resulting in a loss of nitrogen.

When the ground is hard with frost, compost or manure can be barrowed onto plots so it is ready for digging in.

PROTECTION

Any vegetables which look as though they need protecting from severe weather should be attended to right away before they are damaged. This could involve supporting tall vegetables with canes or sticks. In addition, cover any root crops still in the ground, such as parsnips, with straw, bracken or even leaves (held down with netting) to enable you to lift them when the surrounding soil is frozen solid. Leeks also benefit from this treatment.

Cauliflowers, especially the older varieties, can be improved when they are nearing maturity by breaking off an outside leaf and laying it across the curd to protect it from the cold. Lettuces and other vegetables being overwintered in the open can be covered with cloches to help them through the worst weather.

FRUIT

Pruning is one of the main jobs for January but, contrary to what many gardeners might think, it is not a suitable time for pruning all fruits. Raspberries and other cane fruits, for example, should have been pruned in the autumn after fruiting. Currants and gooseberries are best dealt with as soon as the leaves start to fall in the autumn, or in the early spring, and plums and cherries should be pruned in the spring or during the growing season to reduce the risk of infection by the 'silver leaf' fungus disease.

APPLES AND PEARS

Although there are different ways of pruning the younger, and trained trees, the traditional shaped larger trees respond perfectly well to what is called 'regulated' pruning. This method is based on making a small number of larger cuts with a saw, rather than snipping away with secateurs and really doing very little good at all. The tree is really just tidied up rather than pruned. Normally, branches and larger shoots are removed and most young shoots are left alone. Those removed include the dead, dying, or badly diseased. Also prune any branches which are too low, too high, or which spread too wide. Those which are crossing from one side of the tree to the other, and any which are obviously causing overcrowding, must also be removed.

Finally, always remember to treat all saw cuts with a fungicidal paint. This promotes quick healing and helps prevent the entry of diseases.

CANKER

This takes the form of a jagged and cracked wound on a branch or large shoot, the edges being rough and swollen. The damage extends down to the wood, which is laid bare in the centre.

If the disease has spread right round a branch or shoot, the whole piece will have to be cut off below the affected area, because the remaining growth will all be dead. If, however, the disease has not stretched right round the branch, it should be cut out with a knife until you reach healthy bark, and the resulting wound painted with a fungicidal paint. This can be done at the same time as pruning.

STAKING AND TYING

Another winter job involves checking all tree ties and stakes and, if necessary, replacing any damaged ones.

If a tree is quite large and well able to stand without support, a broken stake need not be replaced. However, all tight ties should be loosened or replaced. Also, if a stake is rubbing against a tree and damaging it, the stake should be shortened to prevent such injuries.

PEST CONTROL

A very good and economical method of pest control is to apply a tar oil winter wash while the trees are completely dormant. This will kill the overwintering eggs of many fruit pests, including greenfly. However, since the tar oil can scorch leaves and other tender green tissue, cover all plants under the trees, including the lawn, on which the spray might land.

Mahonia is an outstanding evergreen shrub with magnificent foliage and large heads of fragrant flowers. This is 'Charity' and it will reach 1·2 m (6 ft) or more.

Always apply tar oil *after* pruning – this avoids your getting covered by it as you haul out dead branches.

FEEDING

This is the time of year at which large fruit trees should be fed with a good general fertilizer such as Growmore. By doing it now, the fertilizer will have plenty of time to dissolve and be carried down to the roots, where it is needed, before growth starts in March.

Follow the rates of application on the pack, usually 128 g per m² (4 oz per sq yd) and aim to treat all the ground that is occupied by the root system. Never apply fertilizer as a dressing around the base of the stem or trunk. As a rough guide, the spread of the roots will be very simliar to that of the branches.

PLANTING BUSH FRUIT
If any bare-rooted bushes arrive when the ground is unfit for planting, they should be heeled in temporarily (see **Flowers and shrubs**). If the ground is unfit even for this, leave the plants bundled up in a shed or garage until conditions improve. Plants in containers can be treated in the same way.

STORED FRUIT
Any apples and pears still being stored in cellars, garages, sheds, etc, (see **September, fruit**) must be examined frequently, and any that are showing signs of deterioration should be removed. Those that are ripening should also be taken out as they will only spoil if left.

Above: *Erica herbacea* (*E. carnea*) is a reliable winter-flowering heather that is available in a wide range of flower and foliage colours. Unlike many heathers it will tolerate slightly alkaline soils.

Left: Shrubby dogwoods grown as stools to display their colourful stems include red-stemmed *Cornus alba* 'Sibirica' and yellow-stemmed *C. stolonifera* 'Flaviramea'.

FEBRUARY

FLOWERS AND SHRUBS

Sweet peas need a long growing season if they are to give of their best. Enthusiasts normally sow the seeds in the autumn and overwinter the young plants in frames. You can also sow the seeds now and get successful results.

SOWING SWEET PEAS

Since the seeds are very hard it is a good idea to rub or chip a hole in the outer skin and then soak them in water for a day. Only those which have swollen should be sown. Sow the seeds singly in small pots of sowing or multi-purpose compost, and place them in a frame to speed up germination and to protect the resulting seedlings.

Probably the best pots to use are those made of bitumenized paper, often called sweet pea tubes. They allow the seedlings to grow unchecked because they need not be removed before planting as they rot away in the soil allowing the roots to grow through unhindered.

PLANTING TREES AND SHRUBS

You should nearly have finished planting bare-rooted or root wrapped, deciduous trees and shrubs by now, though it must never be hurried just for that reason. The aim should always be to finish planting before there are any signs of growth.

Prepare the site well, first by digging a hole large enough to accommodate the root system (see illustrations opposite). If the weather is suitably mild and the soil not too wet, container-grown shrubs can be planted in the same way. However, if in doubt, wait a few more weeks for the soil to warm up a little more. The planting of evergreens, conifers and plants growing in containers is covered in **April, flowers and shrubs**.

THE HERBACEOUS BORDER

If the soil and weather are suitable towards the end of the month, being neither wet nor frozen, herbaceous plants may be planted. They are usually bought in plastic bags, with their roots wrapped in peat or moss, or growing in pots.

Prepare the ground well by digging it and, at the same time, incorporating well-rotted garden compost, manure, peat or bark. Before planting, rake in a dressing of a balanced fertilizer such as Growmore, about 64 g per m² (2 oz per sq yd).

The plastic should then be cut away from the plant, with its roots being spread out in the bottom of the specially prepared hole. The soil is then put back over the roots and firmed down, so that the crown of the plant is level with the soil surface when planting is finished.

This is also the time to finish digging any new bed or border, especially if the soil is heavy clay, so the weather has plenty of time to break it up.

CROCUS DAMAGE

Many early flowering spring crocuses will be coming into flower if the weather is kind and they were planted in a sunny position. Sparrows may pick them to bits unless sticks are placed amongst the flowers and black cotton is wound around them. Alternatively treat the flowers, as they start to show colour, with one of the harmless chemical deterrents that are widely available.

LAWNS

February often sees the resumption of worm activity in the lawn after the winter. In mild districts they can be active by the end of the month. Any casts should be swept away. Always remember that worms do help with the drainage of the turf, so they are not really pests.

PLANTS FOR FEBRUARY

Deciduous trees and shrubs			
Alnus glutinosa	Lonicera fragrantissima	Rhododendron	Erythronium (dog's tooth violet)
Chaenomeles	Lonicera purpusii	Sarcococca	Galanthus (snowdrop)
Cornus alba 'Elegantissima' and 'Sibirica'	Magnolia campbellii	Viburnum tinus	Leucojum vernum (snowflake)
	Rubus cockburnianus		
	Salix alba 'Chermesina'	**Climbers**	Species Narcissus
Cornus mas (Cornelian cherry)	Viburnum farreri	Clematis cirrhosa	Scilla (squill)
		Jasminum nudiflorum	
Cornus stolonifera 'Flaviramea'	**Evergreen trees and shrubs**		**Herbaceous perennials**
		Bulbs	Helleborus (hellebores)
Corylus avellana (hazel)	Azara	Anemone blanda	Iris unguicularis (I. stylosa)
Corylus maxima	Camellia	Bulbous irises (I. danfordia, I. reticulata)	Pulmonaria (lungwort)
Daphne mezereum	Daphne		Polyanthus and primulas
Hamamelis (witch hazel)	Garrya elliptica	Crocuses	Violets
	Mahonia	Cyclamen coum	Winter-flowering pansies
	Pieris	Eranthis (winter aconite)	

PLANTING A TREE OR SHRUB

Dig out a hole large enough to accommodate the spread-out root system or the root ball. The depth should be sufficient to allow the soil mark on the stem to be level with the ground. Drive in the stake before planting to avoid damage to the roots.

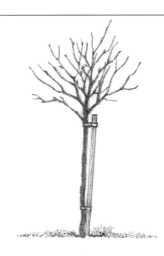

Work plenty of well-rotted garden compost or manure into the bottom of the hole, and also into the earth that has been dug out. In addition a light dressing of Growmore will be beneficial. Tread the soil well in as you fill.

The filling in process is repeated until the hole is full and all the soil has been replaced. In the case of a tree, use tree ties to steady the trunk against the stake. Lean this at a slight angle into the prevailing wind in an exposed site.

Winter aconites (*Eranthis hyemalis*) are tuberous and naturally grow in woodland. Their foliage consists of an attractive ruff of green just below the flower. Plant in humus-rich soil in light shade for best results.

LEAVES AND GENERAL DEBRIS

This must never be allowed to accumulate on the surface of the lawn during the winter as it can smother or weaken the grass causing it to go yellow.

A NEW LAWN

Continue to prepare the site by treading down (not rolling) the surface, and perhaps lightly raking it to create the right tilth. It should, though, only be done when the soil is fit for working.

All digging should have been carried out earlier in the winter to give the land time to settle naturally, so that the new lawn will be level, minus bumps and holes.

Winter-sweet (*Chimonanthus praecox*) can grow to 3 m (10 ft) or more and needs a sunny but sheltered position to thrive. Prune out flowered shoots in spring to just above soil level.

The early digging will also allow the soil to weather, thus ensuring that it will break down into a fine seedbed for a March/April sowing.

MOWING

Something that very few people would contemplate doing in February is mowing the lawn. Even so, it could well be necessary during a mild winter. However, the mower blades should be set to at least 4 cm (1·5 in) high, with the lawn just being 'topped' to keep it tidy and prevent the grass getting too long and matted. In fact one could hardly call it mowing.

VEGETABLES

If you garden on heavy clay soil, you should finish any deep digging as soon as you can so that what remains of the winter weather will break it down into a workable tilth in readiness for sowing and planting. There is not the same urgency with light and sandy soils.

When any previously dug ground has

dried out enough for it to be cultivated, it is always wise to break it down lightly with a fork or hand cultivator, and then cover it with cloches or polythene.

Although, in theory, February is the month in which we can really start gardening again after the winter, this will depend entirely upon the state of the soil and the weather. Even then only the hardiest and large seeded vegetables should be sown. It is wise to protect the ground when it is dry with cloches or polythene tunnels after breaking it down lightly with a fork or hand cultivator. This will keep it dry, and warm it up in readiness for the main sowings next month.

THE FIRST SOWINGS
An early sowing of carrots, lettuces, radishes, salad onions and summer cabbages may be made under cloches or tunnels once the weather shows signs of warming up. Allow 23 cm (9 in) between rows. 'Nantes' carrots can be sown by scattering the seed thinly, not in rows, in a cold frame in the vegetable garden.

Broad beans may be sown in the open when conditions are right. The 'Longpod' and 'Green Windsor' types are the best for sowing now, whereas 'Aquadulce' is the one for the autumn.

Sow the seeds in rows 5 cm (2 in) deep, with 11–12 cm (4.5 in) between seeds, and 45 cm (18 in) between rows. Where space is limited, it is best to grow one of the dwarf varieties, such as 'The Sutton' or the slightly taller 'Feligreen'. Sow the seeds 23 cm (9 in) each way.

Shallots should be planted with the tops just showing above the ground, 15 cm (6 in) apart, with 30 cm (12 in) between rows. The only problem you might encounter is from birds pulling them out of the ground before they have rooted. Hence the need to plant them quite deeply.

VEGETABLES IN SEASON
Many vegetables will still be available for use from the garden and store. Spinach beet, probably some Brussels sprouts, cabbages and savoys and, weather permitting, celery, leeks and parsnips. Those

being stored would include carrots, onions, shallots, swedes and turnips, potatoes and any Dutch white cabbages still hanging up.

RUNNER BEANS
Prepare a deeply dug trench, approximately 60 cm (2 ft) deep, by 1 m (3½ ft) wide, filling it with a good mix of soil and bulky organic matter (compost or manure). This can be done now in readiness for sowing or planting the beans later on. Runner beans are usually grown in a double row with 15 cm (6 in) between seeds, and 60 cm (2 ft) between the rows.

FRUIT
The January calendar of jobs for fruit applies equally well to February. However, there are quite a number of additional tasks which need to be carried out toward the end of the month, as we get the first hint of spring.

PEACHES AND NECTARINES
These may well start into growth now if they are in a warm position against a sunny wall. Once this happens, be on your guard to protect the tender new growth, and later the blossom, against frost.

Not only will the frost check or kill the new shoots, so that they have to start all over again later in the season, but it will also kill the flowers, so ruining any prospect of fruit for the coming season.

The easiest way to prevent frost damage to early new growth is by draping netting over the trees whenever it looks as though a frost is likely. You will be surprised at just how much protection this gives. There is also an ultra-lightweight sheet made especially for the job, called Harvest Guard.

PEACH LEAF CURL
This distorts and reddens the developing leaves, which will fall well before the autumn. The disease also weakens the tree

The symptoms of peach leaf curl are distinctive. This disease can severely weaken a tree. Spray with copper fungicide now and after leaf fall.

Shrubby *Daphne mezereum* may reach 1·5 m (5 ft). It grows well on limy soils. The fragrant flowers are followed by poisonous berries.

HYBRID CANE FRUITS

Tayberries, loganberries, etc, which were tied up in bundles in the autumn, can now be cut free and trained to their wires.

Use a training system that allows the new canes, which will grow during the year, to be tied in loosely and separately from the fruiting ones. The best method is to train the canes to wires stretched between posts or along a wall or fence. These could be 1, 1·2, 1·5, and 2 m (3½, 4, 5 and 6½ ft) high. The top wire is kept for the new canes which will grow up the middle of the plant. The canes which are about to fruit are therefore tied to the bottom three, on each side of the plant.

STRAWBERRIES

At the end of the month you can start forcing strawberries. For the best results, it does mean that the plants should have been potted into 13 cm (5 in) pots last autumn. Do not try to pot them now.

Those already in pots, or other suitable containers, can be brought into a greenhouse (heated or cold) for advancing. With little or no heat, strawberries can be ready for picking by late May. Plants already in rows in the garden may also be brought forward by covering them with either cloches or a polythene tunnel. These will not fruit quite as early, but they will still be well ahead of uncovered plants.

Spread a thick layer, about 10 cm (4 in) deep, of well-rotted garden compost or manure when the soil is moist, and after any pruning has been completed.

enormously and will, within a few years, stop it carrying any fruit. A spray of copper fungicide when the new shoots are about 2–3 cm (1 in) long, followed by another in the autumn straight after leaf-fall, will prevent infection.

FEEDING AND MULCHING

Whereas January was the month for feeding large fruit trees, February is the time for smaller ones, 3–4·5 m (10–15 ft) high. There is no need to be too precise about the timing, for you merely want to give the fertilizer a chance to dissolve and be carried down to the root zone. As in January (see pages 12–13), the balanced fertilizer Growmore can be sprinkled on at about 128 g per m² (4 oz per sq yd) or the rate recommended on the pack.

Mulching beneath young trees and bush fruits, and between rows of cane fruits, can be enormously beneficial because it ensures that the soil retains plenty of moisture.

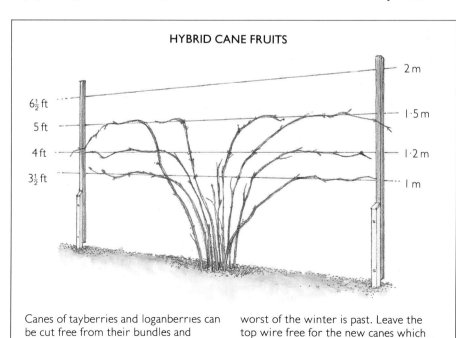

HYBRID CANE FRUITS

6½ ft — 2 m
5 ft — 1·5 m
4 ft — 1·2 m
3½ ft — 1 m

Canes of tayberries and loganberries can be cut free from their bundles and trained along supporting wires now the worst of the winter is past. Leave the top wire free for the new canes which will develop during spring and summer.

MARCH

FLOWERS AND SHRUBS

March is the dividing month between winter dormancy and spring growth. It is also the end of the planting season for deciduous and bare-rooted trees and shrubs, though container-grown stock can be planted virtually all the year round.

All planting should be finished before there are signs of growth. If delayed beyond this point, the plants receive a shock to their system which will result in a check to their growth.

PRUNING

Flowering shrubs that will flower on the coming season's growth should be pruned now. This normally covers those shrubs that flower after about mid summer, and includes buddleia, late flowering ceanothus and clematis, hardy fuchsias, hebes and hydrangeas.

Roses All except ramblers should be pruned now. The old-fashioned shrub roses will really only need tidying up by the removal of old and worn out branches. Floribundas will need harsher treatment, and hybrid teas (HT) even harder pruning.

HTs should be cut back to within 15–30 cm (6–12 in) of the ground to encourage strong new flower-bearing shoots to form. Old, crossing, and weak branches

Hybrids of *Crocus chrysanthus* come in a range of colours including mauve, lilac, yellow and cream. All crocuses need sun to open wide their blooms.

should be removed completely. Floribunda roses are, in principle, treated in the same way, except that the branches are pruned back less severely, by 30–60 cm (1–2 ft). Varieties of climbing rose are pruned slightly differently. All the main branches are retained and tied in to the supports while side shoots are cut back to less than 15 cm (6 in) long.

Winter flowering shrubs These should be pruned to give them the maximum length of time to grow and produce shoots for the next flowering season. Well-known examples of such plants are winter jasmine, witch-hazel, winter-flowering viburnums, winter-sweet (*Chimonanthus*) and flowering heath (*Erica herbacea,* still frequently referred to by its previous name of *E. carnea*).

Winter jasmine is pruned by tying in all the long shoots that you want to retain, and cutting back to 2–5 cm (1–2 in) all the others that have flowered.

PLANTS FOR MARCH

Deciduous trees and shrubs	Evergreen trees and shrubs	Climbers	Narcissus
Chaenomeles (flowering quince)	*Azara*	*Clematis armandii*	*Scilla* (squill)
Cornus mas (cornelian cherry)	*Berberis linearifolia*	**Bulbs**	Tulips
Daphne	*Camellia* (many cultivars)	*Anemone blanda*	**Herbaceous Perennials**
Forsythia	*Erica herbacea* (many cultivars)	*Chionodoxa*	*Bergenia*
Magnolia campbellii	*Daphne*	*Cyclamen coum*	*Doronicum*
Magnolia stellata	*Mahonia*	*Eranthis* (winter aconite)	*Helleborus* (hellebores)
Parrotia persica	*Pieris*	*Erythronium* (dog's tooth violet)	*Pulmonaria* (lungwort)
Prunus	*Rhododendron*	*Hyacinthus*	*Primula*
Viburnum × *bodnantense*	*Ulex europaeus* 'Plena'	*Iris reticulata*	Polyanthus
	Viburnum tinus	*Leucojum vernum*	Violets
			Winter-flowering pansies

Magnolia stellata is outstanding in spring. This is 'Rosea' whose flowers are tinged with pink. It grows to 1·2 m (6 ft) or more and likes a rich, lime-free soil.

Stools Those shrubs grown for the beauty of their coloured stems in the winter are cut hard back to within about 5 cm (2 in) of the old wood. They include: the dogwoods (*Cornus alba* 'Sibirica', *C. alba* 'Elegantissima' and *C. stolonifera* 'Flaviramea'); *Salix alba* 'Chermesina'; the white-stemmed bramble (*Rubus cockburnianus*); and *Cotinus coggygria* 'Notcutt's Variety' for its purple foliage and stems.

FEEDING
Roses and shrubs should be given a top dressing of Growmore fertilizer early in the month to encourage balanced growth and flowering. Growmore contains equal amounts of the three main plant foods, nitrogen, phosphates and potash. A suitable amount is 96 g per m² (3 oz per sq yd) depending on the shrubs' vigour.

SLUGS
Slugs can be a menace in a damp and mild spring. If you would rather not use slug pellets containing metaldehyde (because of the danger of poisoning pets or young children) there is a paste, similar in consistancy to toothpaste, which is equally effective. A proprietary paper tape, impregnated with metaldehyde, is also good.

The chemical methiocarb is, in fact, a more efficient slug killer, but it is more dangerous than metaldehyde if eaten by birds, pets or children.

The safest and most economical way to use slug pellets is to place a dozen or so under a slate or tile at strategic places around the garden.

PLANT PROTECTION
Flowers and young shoots can easily be damaged in March by frost. You must therefore continue to protect them as described in **February, fruit**. Also check that orange flowered crocuses, in particular, are not attacked by sparrows.

Any early bulbs which have finished flowering and whose foliage is yellowing can, if necessary, be lifted and dried off for replanting in the autumn.

PLANTING
On the more constructive side, gladiolus corms can be planted in a sunny border. Unless they are wanted specifically for cutting, they make grand companions for shrubs. Plant the corms about 10 cm (4 in) below the soil. Beyond digging the ground before planting, no special preparations are needed. However, a dressing of Growmore at 69 g per m² (2 oz per sq yd) after flowering strengthens the corms for the following year.

Many herbaceous plants are now available in bare-rooted, pre-packed form. They start to grow somewhat earlier than those kept outdoors, so planting should be completed this month.

SOWING
A start can also be made on sowing hardy annual flowers in their flowering positions when the soil is in a fit state. But never rush into this job, for more harm than good will result from sowing before conditions are right. Rake the seed-bed to a fine tilth and firm well by treading it down before sowing. Sow the seeds in broad groups rather than dotting them about for a

Bergenia 'Ballawley' has magnificent foliage which acts as good ground cover and colours red in autumn. It likes moist soil and grows well in shade.

bolder result. Also, sow in lines within each group so that hoeing in the early stage is easier. Finally, label each group.

LAWNS

This is the month when grass really starts to grow vigorously.

SCARIFYING AND SPIKING

Most lawns suffer from a build-up of moss in the winter and this is the time to tackle it. The important task is to scarify (rake) the lawn to haul out all the old, dead grass, moss, and rubbish that has almost certainly collected in the sward during the winter. If allowed to remain, this will quickly form a waterproof layer on top of the soil which will prevent rain from reaching the roots in the summer, and which will also form a soggy wet surface.

In the past, hand-raking was the only way of scarifying. It was a tiring and tedious job. Now, electric scarifiers have made it child's play.

Spiking This is another job that should, if necessary, be done now, after scarifying. Its purpose is to correct any compaction in the surface so that water can drain away properly, and air can circulate amongst the roots (see illustration).

If there is little moss visible in the lawn, a plain spring lawn food should be given when signs of growth are seen. This will

Chaenomeles × superba 'Knap Hill Scarlet' is one of the best of the red-flowered ornamental quinces. Best trained against a wall or fence, it thrives equally well in sun or shade and tolerates most soils.

LAWN CARE

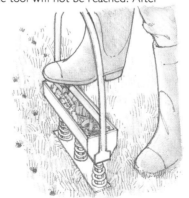

Spring and autumn are the times to aerate the lawn. An ordinary garden fork will do a perfectly adequate job in all but the really bad cases of

compaction, when a hollow-tiner would be more appropriate. Aim to have the rows of holes 10 cm (4 in) apart and make them vertical, or the full depth of the tool will not be reached. After

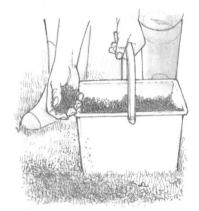

spiking apply a top dressing of sifted soil at the rate of 1 kg per m² (2 lb per sq yd) and brush well in. Then treat the lawn with a combined mosskiller/fertilizer.

Left: Polyanthus come in most colours bar true blue. They have a long flowering season, often starting in winter if the weather is mild. Divide plants after flowering.

Right: Broad beans can be sown this month or in autumn when they will overwinter as young plants.

act as a tonic after the winter and, together with the other treatment recommended, will put the lawn back on its feet.

TURFING AND SOWING

This is one of the main times of the year for turfing. The soil is warming up but will still stay damp for several weeks yet, thus ensuring a good start for the new lawn. However, if the ground is soaking wet or frozen, you must wait until conditions improve. Alternatively, you can wait until the early autumn when the soil is warmer, and a full account of the procedure will be found in **October, lawns**.

Late in the month, preparations for sowing should be completed. Full details of all the earlier work will be found in **February, lawns**. All that now remains is for the surface to have a final raking and levelling, so that the tilth is ready to receive the seed.

Immediately before raking apply a dressing of fine bark or peat at the rate of 268 g per m² (1½ lb per sq yd) particularly if the ground consists of heavy clay. This will greatly aid germination and increase the likelihood of success.

Once the grass is growing, prepare the surface for mowing by brushing and lightly rolling it. The first few mowings should be higher than you would normally cut so that the grass is not subjected to a sudden and vicious attack, which could well damage it. Set your blades at a height of 3 cm (1 in). Don't go any lower.

VEGETABLES

Unless you live on a light, sandy soil, all digging should have been finished by now. Light soil can usually be dug, and compost incorporated, immediately before you cultivate it, though do check it has been well trodden down to prevent water loss by evaporation or very quick drainage. The only exception applies to land that is intended for root vegetables. This should not have compost added because it can encourage the roots to 'fang', producing two or more growing points per root.

VEGETABLES IN SEASON

The first batch of the year should soon be ready for harvesting. This may well include spinach beet and possibly purple sprouting broccoli. Some early spring greens may even be approaching readiness. However, root vegetables (carrots, swedes, etc) in store will soon be spoiling, so eat them up before long.

FEEDING AND HOEING

Spring cabbages sown last August will soon benefit from a feed. A compound fertilizer high in nitrogen will be most effective. Failing that, apply sulphate of ammonia on its own at 32 g per m² (1 oz per sq yd). Hoe in fertilizers if possible, and then, if the ground is dry, water in.

Hoe the ground at first sight of seedling weeds or, if the land is too wet, delay it until drier conditions prevail.

Camellia 'Donation' needs a lime-free soil and a position in light shade to give some protection from late frosts. The blooms are perfection, although they may brown in prolonged spells of wet weather.

SOWING

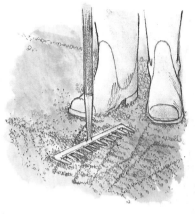

When sowing fine seed sprinkle a little sparingly along the drill.

First rake the soil well to obtain a fine tilth free from large stones. Draw out a drill against a line to ensure the row will be straight.

Cover the seeds; fine seeds need only a light covering. Firm the soil down over the drill. Label the row before you forget!

SOWING

When the weather has begun to warm up, and the soil is sufficiently workable, many vegetables can be sown (see illustration) and planted in the second half of the month. If seeds are to germinate successfully they need warmth (from the sun), moisture (rain) and oxygen (air). When sowing, the first task is to get the tilth sufficiently fine to allow small seeds to grow unimpeded. This is achieved using a hand cultivator and then a rake.

Next, the seed must be buried at the right depth. The depth at which you should sow the seed is nearly always given on the packet but, if in doubt, aim to bury the smaller seeds at a depth of roughly $\frac{1}{2}$ in (13 mm), certainly no deeper.

Beans are easy to sow because they are grown as individual plants and are, therefore, sown individually. Peas are almost as easy because you should aim at six to eight seeds per $0.1\,m^2$ (1 sq ft). Smaller seeds are a little more tricky, but try to average about three seeds per $2.5\,cm$ (1 in) of drill. The art is to have the resulting seedlings well spaced. Sow the following during March in the open: Brussels sprouts, summer cabbage, lettuces, onions, peas, parsnips, broad beans, leeks and many herbs. Always sow thinly in straight rows so that the resulting seedlings grow strongly and are sturdy.

Protection When sowing at this unpredictable and often cold time of year, it is a

Cornus mas, the Cornelian cherry, grows to 3·5 m (12 ft). It carries its yellow flowers on bare branches. The leaves, which appear later, colour well in autumn. It tolerates most soils as long as they are moist.

Above: *Narcissus* 'Jack Snipe' is a dainty variety for naturalizing in grass or a mixed border (see September).

Right: Sprouting broccoli, like most leafy brassicas, is sown in nursery rows before transplanting. Spears will be ready for picking during winter.

good idea to cover the seed rows with either cloches or polythene tunnels to keep the ground warm and prevent rain from wetting it too much. Once the seedlings are emerging strongly above the soil, remove the covering to prevent them becoming weak and drawn.

TRANSPLANTING

When seedlings later need to be transplanted, you should sow only a few seeds at a time. Remember that a 60 cm (2 ft) row can yield food for an entire season!

Vegetables grown in this way include brassicas (cabbage, cauliflower, Brussels sprouts, broccoli, kale, savoy), early lettuces, celery and celeriac, leeks, tomatoes, sweet corn, marrows, and cucumbers.

Those which should always be grown *in situ* (where they are to flower) include beetroot, carrots, swedes, turnips, summer and autumn lettuces, parsnips, radishes, potatoes, shallots, spinach.

PLANTING

Plant out onto their final positions frame-raised summer cabbages sown last month and autumn-sown cauliflowers. Both should be planted firmly. Use a dibber to plant cabbage.

Plant onion sets 10–15 cm (4–6 in) apart with 30–40 cm (12–16 in) between rows. The sets should be planted with the tops only just showing above the soil surface so that starlings, etc, are less likely to pull them out of the ground. Keep an eye on the sets, replanting any that the birds do haul out of the ground.

Early potatoes should be planted 30 cm (1 ft) apart with 60 cm (2 ft) between rows. Be ready to protect them from frost once they have developed shoots.

FRUIT

Planting all bare-rooted trees, bushes and canes should be completed before growth starts towards the end of this month. Those sold in containers can, of course, be planted more or less at any time, though the dormant season (November–March) is still the best time.

PRUNING

Tree and bush fruits, and autumn raspberries, must be pruned by the end of the month. The raspberries are pruned by cutting the old fruited canes right down to the ground. The pruning of apple and pear trees is covered in **January, fruit**; that of bush fruits, in **November**.

The last trees to be pruned should be plums so that the risk of their being infected with 'silver leaf' fungus is reduced to a minimum. This disease normally results in the slow death of the tree.

In country areas, leave the pruning of red currants and gooseberries until just before growth starts in the spring. Bullfinches will often feed on the fruit buds during the winter, and late pruning will allow you to see just which and how many buds have been left. If you still have hybrid cane fruits (tayberries, etc) tied in bundles for winter protection, release them and train them into the wires.

STRAWBERRIES

Because the flowers of perpetual fruiting strawberries are not removed until the end of May, so that fruiting is delayed until the autumn, the plants will still produce a large first season crop if planted now. Aromel is a particularly good variety. Plant all strawberries about 40–50 cm (16–20 in) apart with 75–90 cm (2½–3 ft) between rows.

FROST PROTECTION

This is more important in March than February because more fruits will have started into growth. Obviously, as we go into April and May, the need for vigilance becomes even greater.

The simplest form of protection, as has already been mentioned, is to drape polythene or netting over bushes and small trees at night when frost threatens, removing them in the morning.

FEEDING

Small fruit trees, and all bush and cane fruits, should be given a top dressing of Growmore early in the month. Apply it at 96 g per m² (3 oz per sq yd). Treat the entire ground occupied by the root system, which will be equal to the area covered by the branches.

WEEDING

Although hoeing and hand-weeding are normally effective amongst garden fruit crops, it is sometimes helpful to use a short-term herbicide to kill existing weeds if either a large area is involved, or the ground remains wet and impossible to hoe for long periods.

This is particularly necessary with bush and cane fruits because hoeing can also damage the surface roots unless done with care. A weedkiller containing glyphosate should be used for perennial weeds, but one based on paraquat and/or diquat is quicker for annuals.

PESTS AND DISEASES

They will both be on the increase now. Never be caught out by ignoring or not seeing an attack, because it will soon build up to an uncontrollable level.

Greenfly, capsids, caterpillars, big bud mite on black currants, sucker, and the fungus diseases scab and mildew, may all be seen on a number of fruits. Most of the leading garden chemical manufacturers produce exellent identification charts showing the problem and cure. This eliminates the 'pot-luck' element of trying out different chemicals in the hope of finding the right one.

The use of chemicals should always be kept to a minimum, and they must never be applied simply for the sake of it. No matter what precautions are taken, chemicals never benefit the environment.

Above: Onion sets, like shallots and garlic, should be planted in drills and covered so only the tips of the sets are visible above the soil surface.

Right: Potatoes are planted in deep drills. It is a good idea to put a layer of peat or well rotted garden compost at the bottom as this will lessen the chance of scab developing.

APRIL

FLOWERS AND SHRUBS

April is probably the first month of the gardening year for most domestic gardeners. The weather should be well and truly improving, and the time has come to sow and plant a huge range of ornamental plants and vegetables.

ANNUALS

Hardy annuals are the main flowers to be sown now. Choose a still day because the seeds will be sown in rows and too much wind will blow the finer ones all over the place. Most hardy annuals will be sown *in situ*, and are often used to fill up gaps in developing shrub borders or to add colour to mixed borders. Where space permits, though, sow them to create their own show in a border consisting of drifts and groups of the different flowers.

This annual border should first be planned and marked out, and then the seeds sown in lines in the pre-arranged groups each flower.

HERBACEOUS PERENNIALS

Seeds of herbaceous plants may also be

Leopard's bane, *Doronicum plantagineum*, is one of the first of herbaceous perennials to come into flower.

sown now. Instead of sowing the seeds in their final positions, raise them in nursery rows, and for ease, in the vegetable garden. Sow thinly and plant the resulting seedlings in nursery rows about 30 cm (1 ft) apart when they are about 10 cm (4 in) tall. Plant them out in the late summer or autumn.

If you have a frame to sow in, this will give you larger plants more quickly, and many will flower in the same year. You can sow either direct into the ground or into pots or trays.

HALF-HARDY FLOWERS

They too can be sown now, but only under a frame or cloche because they will be killed by any but the lightest of frosts. It is

---

PLANTS FOR APRIL

Deciduous trees and shrubs	Evergreen trees and shrubs		
Amalanchier	*Berberis* (barberries)	*Clematis armandii*	'Florepleno' (double daisy)
Chaenomeles (flowering quince)	*Camellia*	**Bulbs**	*Bergenia*
Cytisus	*Ceanothus rigidus*	*Allium neapolitanum*	*Cheiranthus* (wallflowers)
Forsythia	*Daphne*	*Anemone*	*Doronicum*
Magnolia	*Osmanthus × burkwoodii*	*Convallaria majalis* (lily-of-the-valley)	*Helleborus corsicus* (*H. argutifolius*)
Malus (crab apple)	*Pieris*	*Crocus* (large flowered)	*Helleborus orientalis*
Prunus (ornamental cherries)	*Rhododendron* (many species and cultivars)	*Erythronium* (dog's tooth violet)	*Myosotis* (forget-me-not)
Rhododendron (many species and cultivars)	*Rosmarinus officinalis* (rosemary)	*Fritillaria* (fritillary)	*Polygonatum*
Ribes (flowering currant)	*Skimmia japonica*	*Muscari* (grape hyacinth)	*Primula*
Spiraea × arguta	*Vinca* (periwinkle)	*Narcissus*	Polyanthus
Spiraea prunifolia		*Scilla* (squill, bluebell)	*Pulmonaria* (lungwort)
Viburnum carlesii	**Climbers**	Tulips	In addition, many alpine and rock garden plants flower in April.
	Clematis alpina	**Herbaceous perennials**	
		Bellis perennis	

more economical to space sow as shown right. Once they have germinated, give them all the ventilation you can, provided that it is reasonably warm.

TREES AND SHRUBS

This is one of the best times of year for planting conifers and evergreen trees and shrubs. The soil is getting warmer every day and the roots will soon start to grow.

The main planting procedure is the same as that described in **February, flowers and shrubs** for bare-rooted subjects. The difference, though, is that the rootball should not be disentangled or the roots spread out. Leave them as found.

Note that those growing in containers (including deciduous plants now in leaf) may, in theory, be planted all the year round, provided that the soil is in a fairly

workable condition and not waterlogged, frozen, or dry and hard.

Prepare the site well by adding plenty of bulky organic matter (well-rotted garden compost or manure) to the soil. Plant firmly and make sure that there is no lack of water during the first, vital, growing season. In windy gardens, protect newly planted shrubs by surrounding them with special windbreak netting.

MULCHING

In drier localities, and on sandy soils, mulching the ground beneath and between shrubs and herbaceous plants helps

Aubrieta and golden *Alyssum saxatile* are easy-to-grow rock plants that tumble brightly down a wall or over the front of a raised bed. Trim over both these plants after flowering.

SPACE SOWING

Space sow half-hardy annuals in groups of two or three seeds, 5–8 cm (2–3 in) apart. They can soon be thinned out in the border in late May.

greatly in reducing stress from lack of water. Providing the soil is damp, the mulch slows down the rate of evaporation from the surface, as well as adding organic matter to the soil, thus further improving its water holding capacity.

One of the best materials for mulching amongst ornamental plants is pulverized bark. It is organic, lasts a long time, does not blow about, and is pleasant to look at. A coarse grade of peat is also first rate, especially amongst acid loving heathers and rhododendrons.

PROTECTION AND DEAD HEADING

Frost protection for tender flowers is still necessary. As previously described, place netting over likely victims on cold nights.

Once daffodil and other narcissus flowers have begun to wither, pick off the dead heads. Not only do they look untidy but, if allowed to produce seeds, the bulbs will be weakened. Never remove the foliage, though, while it is still green and healthy. It feeds the bulb and builds up its energy reserve for next year. Allow about six weeks from the end of flowering before removing the foliage and, preferably, leave it until it has started to turn yellow.

PRUNING HEDGES AND SHRUBS

Evergreen and conifer hedges can be clipped now. This is also the best time to cut back hard into any hedge (deciduous,

evergreen and conifer) that is getting top-heavy, bare at the base, or simply too tall. Such treatment gives the hedge the entire growing season to recover and to make itself presentable again. Any shrubs that have just finished flowering, such as forsythia, may now be pruned so new flowering shoots will have time to develop for next year.

PLANT CARE

Keep seedlings free of weeds using the hoe at first sign of trouble. This is also the time for introducing new water plants to ponds. With the temperature rising, growth will soon start and the new plants will quickly

become established. Pests and diseases, especially greenfly, could be building up by now. Keep a sharp eye open, and act quickly and appropriately to prevent them doing any damage.

LAWNS

Mowing is certainly the most important aspect of April lawn care. The first three or so mowings of the season, as mentioned last month, should be with the blade set higher than usual (on a domestic lawn, about $4\,cm/1\frac{1}{2}$ in). This can be reduced in easy stages so that, by the end of the month, it should seldom be lower than

Above: This is the time of the year to apply a mulch around ornamental plants provided the soil is adequately moist.

Left: A traditional bedding display of tulips underplanted with pale yellow wallflowers (*Cheiranthus*).

about 3 cm (1 in), and never less than 2 cm (¾ in). Only the finest quality lawns will need to be shorter.

SOWING A NEW LAWN

The main preparations were described in **February** and **March, lawns**. The final act now involves raking to achieve a fine tilth and firm surface, free of all but the smallest stones. On no account should the area be cultivated any deeper than by raking, and it must never be rolled. It is then marked out in strips 1 m (3½ ft) wide.

The type of seed mix to buy will depend on what kind of lawn you want. In practice this means that the heavier the wear it will receive, the more ryegrass there should be in the mix. Most domestic lawns should therefore contain a percentage of ryegrass.

Calculate the amount of seed needed for each strip on the basis of 48 g per m² (1½ oz per sq yd), and put the right amount in a tin or jar at the end of each strip. Sprinkle the seed evenly over each strip until the whole lawn is sown. The seed is then raked in lightly and, if the soil is dry and rain is not expected, the area should be thoroughly watered. Take great care to do this gently so that the surface is not puddled and beaten down.

Signs of germination should be seen in one or two weeks, according to the mildness of the weather. Cats and birds can be kept at bay either by a layer of twiggy sticks, netting, or by treating the area with one of the harmless chemical deterrents based on aluminium ammonium sulphate.

TURFING

You should be pressing on with turfing before the warmer weather arrives. If the turves have not rooted into the underlying soil by then, they will have difficulty in doing so unless abundant water is applied.

If gaps are appearing between previously laid turves they should quickly be filled in with sifted soil, and the whole area given a thorough watering. When the turves are not rooting, and shrinking in size, the reason behind the problem is nearly always a lack of water.

LAWN REPAIRS

Any worn patches on existing lawns should be repaired by a sowing of seeds, so that they are well established before the lawn is regularly used in the summer. The

Anemone blanda is a small, tuberous woodland plant available in white and shades of pink, as well as the familiar blue of the species.

bare soil should be vigorously raked or lightly pricked over with a fork to loosen the surface. Sprinkle on some seed mixed with sifted soil, and water in well.

Any lawn edges in need of repair should also be dealt with now (see illustration).

TACKLING LAWN PROBLEMS

Moles can be a nuisance in lawns both now and in the autumn. There are no easy ways of getting rid of them.

Pushing mature bramble or rose shoots into the runs may deter them as will chemical deterrents. But the moles may merely move to another part of the garden! Leatherjackets will be re-appearing after the winter's inactivity. These are the larvae of the daddy-long-legs (crane fly), and they feed below the surface of the lawn on the roots of the grass. This often leads to small patches of dead grass. The presence of lots of starlings on a lawn is

---

REPAIRING LAWN EDGES

Move the cut turf forwards so the damaged edge can be cut away. The resulting patch of bare earth can be filled with sieved compost and seeded.

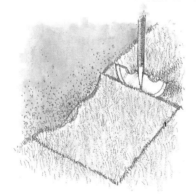

The first thing to do when repairing a lawn edge is to cut out a square of turf around the damaged area.

Left: Sweetly scented lily-of-the-valley (*Convallaria majalis*) is a useful ground coverer in a shady spot.

Above: *Magnolia × soulangiana* is one of the glories of the spring. In a rich, lime-free soil it grows to 1·5 m (5 ft).

usually a good indication that there are leatherjackets about. There is at least one proprietary lawn pest killer available that will control them.

VEGETABLES

In most springs this is an even busier month than last because it is usually only now that the soil is in a fit condition for cultivating and sowing.

SOWING

Any of the seeds that were recommended for sowing in March can be sown in April. These include Brussels sprouts, summer cabbage, lettuces, onions, peas, parsnips, broad beans, leeks and various herbs. Remember to sow thinly in straight rows so that the resulting seedlings grow unimpeded and strongly.

In addition, the following half-hardies (runner beans, French beans, celery, sweet corn, courgettes and marrows) may be sown under cloches or polythene tunnels towards the end of the month. This will protect them from frost and also ensure

early maturity. If you want them to mature where they are, sow them in the ground. However, if they are to be transplanted as young plants, sow them into individual small pots containing a seed or multi-purpose compost.

The following may be sown outdoors in the open: beetroot, cabbages, carrots (protect them with a soil insecticide against carrot fly), pickling and salad onions, turnips, leeks, lettuces, peas, radishes and spinach. Many of these vegetables have been mentioned before and will be referred to again. This indicates that they may be sown over quite a long period to produce either a succession of crops throughout the season, or just one sowing at any time during the recommended period.

POTATOES

Maincrop potatoes should be planted in drills 10–13 cm (4–5 in) deep, allowing 40 cm (16 in) between tubers and 70 cm (28 in) between rows.

Try not to be tempted into growing too many maincrop potatoes if space is limited. They take up a lot of room and can

be bought quite cheaply. Concentrate on the more expensive or less easily found types of vegetable.

HARVESTING

Keep up to date with harvesting and using mature vegetables. Never let them spoil by leaving them in the ground when they are past their best. Do not be tempted to wait until they are that little bit bigger; they will probably only deteriorate.

If the spring has been a good one as regards the weather, lettuces sown in frames last October should be approaching maturity.

CARING FOR SEEDLINGS

Keep an eye on any half-hardy seedlings from earlier sowings, and be ready to protect them from frost. The simple way of doing this is to put newspaper or paper sacks over the frames or tunnels any evening when a frost threatens. Remember to weight them down, though, or they could end up all over the garden! Also, be sure to remove the covering in the morning so that the plants get full light.

WEED PROBLEMS

If vegetable seedlings are growing well, think how much better weed seedlings will be flourishing. You must always keep on top of the hoeing whenever the weather permits. Half-an-hour with the hoe on a dry day will save hours of work later on.

If weeds begin to grow in areas that are too wet to be hoed successfully, a thick mulch of garden compost or bark could be used to smother them. Even a sheet of black polythene works well but, as with newspaper mentioned earlier, it must be weighted down to stop it blowing about. If the worst comes to the worst, you will have to weed by hand.

FRUIT

Most of the popular commonly grown fruit trees and bushes will now be in flower. Black currants and red currants, gooseberries, plums and cherries, and most pears all flower during April, but a night frost shortly before, during or after blossom will usually spell disaster and rule out the chances of fruit the coming season. Apples usually blossom in the first half of May, and are therefore less at risk.

FROST PROTECTION

This is where one of the main benefits of growing small fruit trees and bush fruits comes in as they can more easily be protected from spring frosts than large trees. The simplest way is to drape netting or even polythene over the trees and bushes on evenings when frost threatens. The signs are usually easy to interpret. On calm and cloudless evenings, even following warm and sunny days, the temperature can drop to freezing point and below. There are very rarely frosts when there is good cloud cover.

STRAWBERRIES

Any strawberries that are being covered to produce early crops must be ventilated whenever the weather is warm (this could mean every time the sun is shining). If it gets too hot under the cloches or tunnels, the plants will suffer. Another danger comes from pests and diseases. When they appear on covered strawberries they should be dealt with promptly. A spray containing permethrin is a very good all-round treatment but chemicals for greenfly control are available that will not kill bees and other beneficial insects.

Perpetual fruiting strawberries

Such varieties as 'Aromel', 'Gento' and 'Ostara', which are wanted for autumn fruiting, are best de-blossomed until the end of May. This will stop them fruiting at the same time as the summer varieties. Remember too that there is no such thing as a strawberry which only fruits in the autumn; it is simply a perpetual fruiting variety that is de-blossomed until the end of May.

PESTS AND DISEASES

With all the activity going on in the garden during April, pests and diseases can sometimes be way down the list of priorities. This is definitely a mistake.

With fruit in particular, if a plant is attacked or infected and damaged this early in the season, it can ruin the crop completely. Unlike, say, lettuces, you only have one chance a year with fruit. The ones to look out for are greenfly, capsid bugs, caterpillars, big bud mite on black currants, scab and mildew (mainly on apples and pears).

Try to avoid spraying any fruit during the blossom-period because many beneficial insects will perish.

Left: Cordon pears covered in blossom will need protection overnight when frost threatens.

Above: 'Kiku-shidare-Sakura' or Cheal's Weeping cherry tolerates limy soils.

MAY

FLOWERS AND SHRUBS

One of the main jobs in the flower garden is to harden off and plant out all the hardy and half-hardy bedding plants that you have been raising under glass. The actual time for planting will vary with where you live but, as a guide, the second half of the month is usually safe for the southern half of England whereas, in the north and Scotland, you normally have to wait until June to avoid all danger of frost.

HARDENING OFF

The way to harden off plants is to give them progressively cooler conditions until they become used to outside temperatures. This can be achieved by giving the plants ever more ventilation in the greenhouse or frames or, if they have been raised indoors, by putting them outside during all but the coldest days and bringing them in at night. Hardening off should continue over a ten-day period.

Never be tempted to buy or plant out half-hardy subjects too early. You may run the risk of having them killed or checked by frost and, at best, they will need protecting. However, it is perfectly in order to buy and stand them in a cold frame until it is safe to plant.

CLEANING THE BORDERS

Before any replanting of borders can take place, the spring bedding plants will have to be cleared. Wallflowers, etc, can go on the compost heap, but tulips, hyacinths and other bulbs should be lifted, dried off and saved. They are not normally used as bedding bulbs again because many will not be big enough to flower the following year. However, they are very useful for brightening up a dull corner.

CONTAINERS

Window boxes, tubs and hanging baskets should also be planted up. The aim should be to provide instant colour so the plants must be well in bud or actually flowering when they are planted.

Usually the best potting composts for containers are the peat-based ones, as they are much lighter than those containing loam. An exception to this might be where tall and more permanent plants, such as standard fuchsias or even young trees, are being grown outdoors in tubs. There, the greater weight of a loam-based compost adds stability to the container and provides a stronger root-hold.

DAHLIAS AND EARLY FLOWERING CHRYSANTHEMUMS

This is the time to plant out these flowers. The site should be thoroughly dug and well enriched with bulky organic matter (well-rotted garden compost, etc). Just before planting, a dressing of general fertilizer, such as Growmore, should be given at the recommended rate.

As both these plants need the support of a cane or stake, the latter should be pushed in the ground after the hole has been dug but before the plant has been settled in.

HARDY ANNUALS

Those that were sown last month *in situ* will need thinning soon after the seedlings are large enough to handle to avoid any risk of overcrowding and consequent weakening. There is no need to stick rigidly to the recommended distances on the pack – they are only there as a guide. The important point is to retain the best and strongest plants.

PLANTS FOR MAY

Deciduous trees and shrubs

Cercis siliquastrum (Judas tree)
Crataegus (hawthorn, May)
Cytisus
Deciduous azaleas
Deutzia gracilis
Genista
Kerria
Kolkwitzia (beauty bush)
Laburnum
Magnolia
Prunus padus (bird cherry)
Spiraea
Syringa (lilac)
Tamarix tetranda
Tree peony
Viburnum opulus
Viburnum plicatum

Evergreen trees and shrubs (see also **April**)

Buddleia globosa
Ceanothus
Choisya ternata (Mexican orange blossom)
Cistus × corbariensis
Erica (heathers)
Evergreen azaleas

Climbers

Clematis alpina
Clematis macropetala
Clematis montana
Wisteria

Bulbs

Allium
Anemone
Convallaria majalis (lily-of-the-valley)
Erythronium (dog's tooth violet)
Fritillaria (fritillary)
Hyacinthus (hyacinth)
Leucojum aestivum (snowflake)

Herbaceous perennials

Aquilegia
Bellis perennis
Centaurea
Cheiranthus (wallflowers)
Dicentra (bleeding heart)
Doronicum
Euphorbia (spurge)
Geranium (hardy)
Iris
Paeonia (peony)
Polygonatum
Saxifraga umbrosa
Trollius (globe flower)
Viola (various)

Any gaps that you find along the rows can usually be filled with strong thinnings. After thinning, give the seedlings a really good watering to settle them in and to help them recover from the upheaval.

SUPPORT

Herbaceous plants which are going to grow to more than about 30 cm (1 ft) high should be supported when they are still only several centimetres tall. If it is done with twiggy pea sticks, subsequent growth will quickly hide them. Plants that need supporting in this way include Michaelmas daisies, border phlox, and delphiniums. The latter may need to have the individual stems supported by canes. Hardy annuals may also benefit from this method of support, but not those used for formal bedding. If you have chosen suitable and traditional types, they will be sturdy enough to be self-supporting.

SOWING

Continue sowing herbaceous plants in nursery rows outdoors. Also, many of next spring's bedding plants can be sown now

Above: *Viburnum opulus* 'Sterile' (snowball tree), golden flowered laburnum and *Viburnum plicatum* in the foreground; all three grow well in limy soils.

Left: Growing to 1 m (3½ ft) or so, *Cistus × corbariensis* flowers in May and June. It thrives in a hot, dry position.

including wallflowers, forget-me-nots, and polyanthus. The vegetable plot is the most convenient place for them, because they can be sown in rows along with everything else, later being transplanted singly into wider rows with no difficulty.

The final category that needs sowing involves hardy annuals in readiness for an autumn display. Although the main sowing was in March or April, those plants will finish flowering at the height of summer. A sowing now will extend the display well into the autumn.

FINISHING TOUCHES

Never allow weeds to become established, especially amongst annuals and bedding plants. They will soon overtake and ruin them unless you keep the hoe going.

May is also the best time to lift, split up and replant any alpines which have finished flowering and which are showing signs of becoming worn out. This is usu-

ally revealed by the flowers becoming fewer and smaller, and growth being reduced. Bits may even start dying off.

Finally, continue pruning any ornamental shrubs that have finished flowering so they can produce more flowering shoots next year.

LAWNS

The most important job this month is to treat any weeds in the lawn with an appropriate weedkiller. If tackled now, they should die well before they flower and spread their seeds.

MOWING

Mowing will be in full swing now, being carried out regularly and frequently. Once a week is normal for most domestic lawns, but it can easily be more in a warm, wet spring when grass is growing quickly. A regular mowing ensures that the grass is

cut at more or less the same stage, and to the same height every time.

If you wait until the grass is long before giving it a close cut, it will inevitably be weakened, and this will make way for weeds and moss.

If there are any shallow depressions in the lawn that make it difficult to mow, they should be top-dressed periodically during the early part of the summer. Sprinkle sifted soil into the depression at the rate of about $\frac{1}{2}$ kg per m² (1 lb per sq yd) and brush it well into the sward. Never apply too much soil at any one time or the grass might be smothered.

SCORCHING

Bitches' urine can cause brown marks in the grass. The only cure for a scorched patch is time, but if you can throw water onto the affected area immediately after the dog has fouled it, you will not have any marks to worry about.

Opposite: *Clematis macropetala* has dainty flowers and foliage. The seed-heads are attractive, too, if allowed to form. Cut back after flowering if space is limited but regular pruning is unnecessary.

Left: A perfect lawn is the result of regular care and effort throughout the year. An important aspect of this involves setting the mower blade to the correct height. 'Scalping' will expose bare earth for weeds to germinate and if the cut is too high coarse grasses will be encouraged.

VEGETABLES

From now on new vegetables will be becoming ready for gathering all the time. They include spring cabbages, spring onions which were sown last August, lettuces and radishes.

SOWING

The main crops to be sown in the open this month are the half-hardy runner and French beans, sweet corn, marrows, courgettes and outdoor cucumbers, unless the sowing of these is already under way.

These vegetables will clearly ripen later than plants raised under glass, or garden cloches, but they will still have ample time to produce full crops. Always be ready, though, to protect them from frost, once they are growing.

Sow sweet corn in square groups, rather than rows, to aid pollination and therefore the quality of the cob. Marrows, courgettes and outdoor cucumbers perform best in growing-bags, but any well manured piece of ground will be adequate. Savoys and winter cabbages should be sown in nursery rows for planting out when large enough, in about one month's time.

Further successional sowings can also be made of lettuces and radishes. Meanwhile, maincrop varieties of turnips ('Golden Ball'), carrots ('Chantenay Red Cored' and 'Autumn King') and beetroot ('Cheltenham Mono') should be sown. They will stay in the ground until the autumn when they are lifted and stored.

except cauliflowers should be planted firmly using a dibber.

Cauliflowers are best planted with a trowel to prevent root damage and to encourage quick establishment. Water them in after planting if the soil is at all dry. Transplant when their height (excluding roots) is 10–15 cm (4–6 in); smaller plants will need more looking after, and larger ones will take longer to establish. Protect all these new transplants against cabbage root fly, either with a soil insecticide or a collar of cardboard around the base of the stem.

THINNING
Shortly after seedlings are large enough to handle, thin and single them as necessary. This will apply mainly to root crops such as carrots, beetroot and parsnips, but also

Cauliflowers are best planted with a trowel to keep root disturbance to a minimum. Firm in young plants well and water.

After transplanting it is advisable to protect any young brassica against cabbage root fly. A collar placed round the base of the stem is very effective.

HALF-HARDY VEGETABLES
Any previously mentioned half-hardy vegetables (tomatoes, sweet corn, marrow, courgettes, runner beans, etc) that were sown earlier (see **April, vegetables**) and which are now ready for planting out should first be hardened off (see page 32). They can be planted outside where they are to mature.

TOMATOES
Plant tomatoes 45 cm (18 in) apart with 60 cm (24 in) between rows, marrows and courgettes 60 cm (2 ft) apart, sweet corn 45 cm (18 in) apart and 60 cm (24 in) between rows, and runner beans 15 cm (6 in) apart and 45 cm (18 in) between rows. Those that were raised *in situ* in frames or under cloches will normally only need to

The tree peony, *Paeonia delavayi* var. *lutea*, is an unusual and attractive shrub for the garden. It flowers during May and June and needs a well-drained, loamy soil, but otherwise is quite easy to grow.

be given progressively more ventilation until, finally, the covering is removed altogether and the plants are on their own.

If you are buying tomato plants, choose 'Outdoor Girl' or 'Red Alert' (cherry size) as these are both reliable modern varieties.

BRASSICAS
Many of the brassica seedlings that have been raised in the open, from seed sown in March and early April, will now be ready for planting in their final positions. All

spinach and lettuces. A useful trick with many is to single them to half the recommended distance – eg 10 cm (4 in) instead of 20 cm (8 in) – and then, when the plants are touching each other in the row, thin them further to the full spacing recommended on the packet.

Most thinnings will be perfect for eating young and tender whereas, if originally thinned to the full distance, they would have been wasted. Lettuces and carrots are especially suitable for this treatment.

After thinning any vegetables, always water thoroughly to settle them in and get them growing again. In the case of carrots, this also prevents them from wilting and giving off a strong scent that attracts the damaging carrot fly.

PEAS AND RUNNER BEANS

They should be supported when they are still only several centimetres high, and long before they start to topple over. Peas are best dealt with using either twiggy sticks or purpose-made pea or bean netting.

Runner beans can be supported with the same netting but canes are normally used. They should be 2 m (6½ ft) long, with the bottom being pushed 30 cm (1 ft) into the ground. If the beans are in a double row with 60 cm (2 ft) between the rows, bend the canes over towards each other and tie their tops together for support.

To make the support even stronger, fix more canes along the apex, where the existing canes have been tied together. An alternative system involves growing the beans in a mixed border by the wigwam method which will look decorative.

POTATOES

When potatoes have made about 15 cm (6 in) of top growth, they should be earthed up (see illustration). This will encourage the formation of many more tubers from the underground section of stem and, at the same time, protect the exposed tender growth from being caught by the frost. It will also kill any weeds that might have grown amongst the potatoes. (They can, in fact, be earthed up at any time if you are expecting frosty weather.)

GENERAL TASKS

Continue hoeing to prevent weeds from becoming established.

More or less any non-woody waste

EARTHING UP POTATOES

Use a draw hoe to pull the earth between the rows up and around the top growth. If the tops are short, the soil can be drawn right over to cover the foliage, protecting it from frost.

vegetation can be used to form rich and fertile garden compost for adding to the soil later on.

Finally, keep an eye open for pests and diseases and treat them appropriately as soon as they are seen so they don't have a chance to build up. The most common problem will be greenfly, while some early caterpillars may also be about.

FRUIT

As in April, the main task this month is to prevent frost killing the blossom and developing fruits. Apples are especially susceptible during May. Use the same anti-frost techniques as described in **February, fruit**. The important point is to

Below: *Ceanothus thysiflorus* is one of the evergreen Californian lilacs. Grow in a light well drained soil in a sunny position, preferably against a wall or fence, for success.

remove any covering as early as possible the following morning after the frost has lifted otherwise pollinating insects may not reach the blossom.

STRAWBERRIES

Protecting the blossoms of summer-fruiting strawberries from frost and continuing to remove the flower trusses from perpetuals (autumn fruiting) will remain garden tasks until the end of May.

Strawberry plants that were moved into a cold greenhouse in late February should have fruit ready for picking by the end of the month (an appropriate time because it coincides with the Chelsea Flower Show!). Those plants growing in the open garden, but which were covered with cloches or tunnels in February, may also be fruiting by the end of the month. If less effective coverings than glass were used, June is a more likely date.

GOOSEBERRIES

Other fruits that you could easily be picking by the second half of May are gooseberry thinnings from the bushes of mainly dessert varieties. They are removed to increase the size of the retained berries on the bushes.

Thinning needs to be carried out more than once, as the crop dictates. A heavy crop will need more thinning than a light one. Start by removing alternate berries in May and, if necessary, thin again later on if those retained still appear to be crowded. The thinnings make excellent berries for cooking. Culinary varieties, such as 'Careless', are seldom thinned because the size of the berries is immaterial – quantity is what counts.

PRUNING

Any fruit trees which are being grown in an 'intensive' form (cordons, espaliers, fans, etc) can receive their first summer pruning as soon as the new shoots are several centimetres long. This involves pinching out unwanted shoots. They may be redundant because they are pointing

Spectacular red bracts in spring make *Pieris formosa* var. *forrestii* a memorable sight. This evergreen shrub grows to 2·5 m (8 ft) or more and needs a lime-free soil. Ideal in a heather garden if space permits.

in the wrong direction, causing overcrowding, or are growing straight towards the wall or fence against which the trees are trained.

WEED CONTROL
This is particularly important amongst bush (currants and gooseberries) and cane fruits (raspberries, loganberries, tayberries, blackberries and other hybrid berries), and strawberries.

In an emergency, and amongst young weeds, you may consider using an appropriate weedkiller, such as one containing paraquat and diquat. Used carefully, so that it is kept off all foliage and green

An espalier trained apple. Do not spray when flowers are fully open or pollinating insects will be killed.

shoots, it will kill small weeds quickly and will leave no harmful residues in the soil.

PEST AND DISEASE CONTROL
During May, look out for apple sawfly, gooseberry sawfly, red spider mite, caterpillars and capsid bugs, the last three pests attacking most fruits. Spray only if they become a problem. Also watch out for slugs amongst strawberries.

Strawberries and raspberries have a

particular problem with greenfly because it is responsible for passing virus diseases from one plant to another. There is no cure for a virus disease (the victims should be dug up and burnt) so an insecticide specific to greenfly must be used at the first sign of an infestation.

The other main diseases to look out for this month are mildew and scab on apple and pear trees.

One fungus that is bound to attack strawberries is grey mould (botrytis). It rots the fruit and turns them into little furry puffballs. Spray the plants every fortnight with a systemic fungicide, starting when the first flowers are open.

JUNE

FLOWERS AND SHRUBS

Provide supports for herbaceous plants and hardy annuals as necessary. Harden off and plant out any remaining plants that were raised under protection. While early June is usually the end of the planting out season in southern England, it can still be in full swing in the northern part of the country and in Scotland.

SOWING BIENNIALS

Any biennials that are wanted for next spring's bedding, and herbaceous plants that have not been sown, should go in without delay so that they make large enough plants to withstand the winter. Sow them in rows in the vegetable area and make sure that the ground never dries out before the seedlings are growing strongly. Water them as necessary.

WEED CONTROL

Keep hoeing to keep down weeds amongst any flower beds and borders which have not been mulched.

If residual (persistant) weedkillers (eg simazine-based kinds) were used amongst roses and shrubs in the spring to stop weeds appearing throughout the growing season, you should never hoe the ground unless it is quite clear that weeds are now growing. The disturbance to the soil surface will simply break the 'seal' of herbicide and allow weed seeds to germinate.

PRUNING

Any shrubs that have flowered recently may, if necessary, be pruned now to give them the best chance of producing a really good display next year. In most cases, this will mean reducing any overcrowding and cutting out any branches which are old.

Deadheading This involves removing the dead flower heads of any plants which have either finished flowering or which are now carrying dead flowers amongst living ones. With most flowering plants, dead flowers will soon develop into seed heads. They take a lot of energy from the plants which, in the case of roses, will diminish future flower displays.

When deadheading roses, cut back the whole section that has flowered to a strong bud just below the head. This bud should

ROSE SUCKERS

To remove suckers from a rose, draw back the earth from the base of the plant to expose the point of origin. Then, wearing stout gloves, pull off the sucker. If it is cut away, more suckers will arise from buds around the base.

PLANTS FOR JUNE

Deciduous trees and shrubs
Abutilon
Buddleia alternifolia
Buddleia globosa
Cornus kousa
Deutzia
Genista
Kolkwitzia (beauty bush)
Philadelphus (mock orange, syringa)
Potentilla (shrubby)
Robinia pseudoacacia (locust tree)
Roses
Spiraea × vanhouttei
Syringa (lilac)
Viburnum opulus

Viburnum plicatum
Weigela

Evergreen trees and shrubs
Carpenteria
Ceanothus
Cistus
Cotoneaster
Daboecia (Irish heath)
Kalmia latifolia
Olearia macrodonta
Phlomis fruticosa (Jerusalem sage)
Pyracantha (firethorn)
Rhododendron (hardy hybrids)
Vinca (periwinkle)

Climbers
Clematis (large-flowered hybrids)
Hydrangea petiolaris
Lonicera (honeysuckle)
Roses (climbing)
Wisteria

Bulbs
Allium
Iris (English, Dutch and Spanish)
Lilium (lily)

Herbaceous perennials
Achillea
Anchusa
Aquilegia
Aruncus
Astilbe

Astrantia
Campanula (bell flowers)
Coreopsis
Delphinium
Dianthus (pinks)
Digitalis (foxglove)
Eremurus (foxtail lily)
Geraniums (hardy)
Geum
Iris (bearded)
Lupinus (lupin)
Lychnis
Papaver orientalis (Oriental poppy)
Paeonia (peony)
Polygonatum (knotweed)
Verbascum (mullein)
Violas and pansies

CORRECT   INCORRECT

CLIPPING A HEDGE
The correct way to clip a hedge is to make the top narrower than the bottom. This will add stability and encourage a thick base to form.

be pointing in the direction you want the new shoot to grow. Early flowering herbaceous plants which are deadheaded now will often produce another flush of flowers later in the year.

While deadheading roses, you should always remove any suckers that have grown up from the roots. They are far less common now than they used to be, because modern rootstocks are mainly non-suckering.

After the first blaze of roses, give the bush a chance to rest. This is an excellent time to give a top-dressing of rose fertilizer to encourage further flowering.

Hedges The quick growing types, such as privet and *Lonicera nitida*, will need clipping two or three times a year if they are to stay within bounds and form a dense hedge.

BULBS

Once spring flowering bulbs have finished flowering and then been allowed at least six weeks unhindered growth, the foliage can safely be cut down in the knowledge that the bulbs will flower well again in subsequent years.

Although not essential, clumps of bulbs which have remained in the same place for more than about five years should be lifted and split up. They can either be replanted straight away or dried off and left until the autumn. This treatment greatly improves

Stake tall subjects and remove faded blooms at regular intervals to keep the herbaceous border in trim.

Opposite left: The ball-like flowerheads of bulbous *Allium christophii* can be dried to use in winter flower arrangements. *Viola cornuta* 'Alba' edges the border.

Opposite right: *Lilium regale*, the regal lily, is an undemanding sun-lover for tub or border. This association with annual *Nicotiana* 'Lime Green' is particularly effective.

Left: *Viburnum opulus* 'Sterile' continues to flower during June. The large-flowered *Clematis* 'Lasurstern' has been allowed to scramble through its branches.

the flowering quality and quantity. Be warned, however, that overcrowded bulbs and removal of the foliage too soon after flowering are the main reasons for a reduction in flower displays in subsequent years, so bear this in mind.

SEEDLINGS

Any herbaceous perennial or biennial seedlings that have reached several centimetres high should be lifted and planted in nursery rows, preferably in the vegetable garden. Plant them out 25 cm (10 in) or so apart and water them in well.

When transplanting mixed colours of one sort of plant (eg mixed wallflowers), make sure that you keep all except the tiniest seedlings because some colours produce naturally smaller plants.

FINAL CONSIDERATIONS

Cuttings of pinks and border carnations may be taken now. Snap off leafy shoots (not the longer flowering shoots) that are several centimetres long and push them into a mixture of 50:50 peat and sand in a cold frame or under a cloche. Keep them well watered and they should root in three to four weeks.

When 15–23 cm (6–9 in) tall, the tips of early flowering chrysanthemum plants should be nipped out now to induce side shoots to form. This leads to a far more even, bushy, and productive plant.

Finally, keep on top of all pests and diseases, especially black spot and mildew

on roses. Both can be controlled with a systemic fungicide.

LAWNS

Much of what was said about lawns in May is still applicable in June. If you are planning to sow a new lawn in August or September, finish any deep cultivation soon so that the area has plenty of time to settle naturally. It also gives several months during which it is possible to hoe out any weed seedlings that appear.

DRY WEATHER

Under excessively dry conditions, the height of the mower blades should certainly be raised by 13 mm ($\frac{1}{2}$ in).

Nor will it hurt to allow the mowings to 'fly' during these dry spells – letting them scatter over the lawn instead of collecting them in the grass box. The mowings will act as a mild mulch and go a little way towards stopping excessive surface evaporation and add to the organic matter already in the soil.

Watering This should be done really thoroughly, with a sprinkler, so that the equivalent of at least 2·5 cm (1 in) of water is given at any one application. There are two ways of determining how much water

has been applied to the lawn's surface.

One way is to stand empty tins or jars on the lawn and measure the amount of water that collects in them. The other, and more sophisticated method, is to invest in an inexpensive water meter that you attach to the tap and which cuts off the supply when the pre-set amount has been delivered. This is also an extremely efficient way of watering recently sown or turfed lawns as they should never dry out during their first summer.

WEEDING

Last month was the start of the lawn weeding season. Excellent results can be achieved throughout the summer so long as the grass *and* weeds are growing strongly. If they are not, then you should wait until they are. Lawn weedkillers are absorbed by the leaves of the weeds, not the roots, and the leaves will only absorb a lethal dose if they are young and active.

Lawn weedkillers are of two basic types: those that are applied as granules, and

In the vegetable
garden runner
beans are in flower
and growing fast.
French beans sown
last month and
cabbages planted
out at the same
time are also
growing apace.

those that are watered or sprayed on. The
granular type is invariably a combined
weedkiller/fertilizer which encourages
growth and thereby achieves a better kill
rate. Liquid formulations are available
either as weedkillers alone, as combined
fertilizer/weedkillers, or as a cocktail of
weedkiller/fertilizer/mosskiller.

There is really very little to choose
between the various types except that,
where a serious weed problem exists, such
as clover or daisies, the liquid formulations are marginally more effective
because they give a complete coverage of
the weed leaves; they also tend to be easier
to apply evenly.

Of course, where only a few weeds exist,
one of the several spot-weedkillers is more
economical, or you may be quite happy
just to dig them out with an old table-knife.

Seedheads During June seedheads of
grass often appear. This is perfectly
natural and there is nothing you can do to
stop them forming. They usually defy
cutting by cylinder mowers so it is often
good policy, towards the end of the month,
to slip over the lawn with a rotary mower.
This will cut off all the seedheads. From
then on cylinder mowers will be able to
cope and give a tidy result.

VEGETABLES

Several vegetables may be sown or planted out during the month of June.

SOWING

Sow successive sowings of such crops as
lettuces, radishes, and a final row of peas.
The peas should be of the first early type,
such as 'Early Onward'. They have a
shorter growing season than maincrop
varieties, and will have plenty of time to
mature before the autumn chill sets in.

Suitable varieties (see **May, vegetables**) of carrots, beetroot, swedes and
turnips can all be sown now for lifting and
storing in October. You can also sow
spinach beet now for a very welcome
winter and spring leaf vegetable.

PLANTING OUT

Several vegetables, such as savoys and cabbages, that were sown last month, will be ready for planting out in June. As with lettuces, you can plant these out (using a dibber) at half the recommended distance, ie 23 cm (9 in) instead of 45 cm (18 in), and when the plants are touching, remove and use alternate ones. The thinnings can be used if you wish.

Always transplant when the plants are still small. Older plants suffer a greater check when transplanted and take longer to establish themselves. Also remember to protect all brassica transplants with either a soil insecticide or a cardboard collar to protect them against cabbage root fly (see **May, vegetables**).

In the north, the first half of June is the time for planting out half-hardy vegetables raised under cover. They might include sweet corn, marrows and courgettes, ridge cucumbers, sweet peppers and tomatoes.

Leeks These will now be ready for planting out. Keen leek growers dig out a trench, plant the leeks in the bottom and periodically fill in the trench as the plants grow. By the early winter, the trenches will have been filled level with earth and the leeks have long, blanched stems.

A more 'domestic' way of growing leeks is simply to trim back the root system to a centimetre or so before planting out. Some gardeners also trim back the leaves to give a plant some 20 cm (8 in) long. This can reduce the risk of wilting.

Make a dibber hole about 15 cm (6 in) deep, drop the plant in and fill the hole with water. This will be sufficient to settle the young leek in the ground without any further firming and, over the weeks, it will grow and fill the hole.

TOMATOES

They will need a supporting stake alongside them, whether they be bush varieties or those grown as a single stem. First, dig out the hole for the plant, then push the stake into the bottom, and finally plant the tomato against it. For added strength, pass garden twine down the length of the row securing each cane to it.

An excellent alternative and widely adopted method of growing tomatoes, marrows, courgettes and cucumbers, is in growing bags. The plants in bags will need little attention for the first few weeks, beyond watering. However, when the first fruits start to develop, you will have to start feeding them, about fortnightly to begin with, using a liquid fertilizer formulated to encourage fruit development.

Once side shoots begin to appear in the leaf axils of single stem varieties of tomato (as opposed to bush varieties), they must be nipped out periodically to prevent them developing further and reducing the plant's fruiting abilities.

In exposed gardens, it may be necessary to protect the plants with an improvised screen of windbreak netting, at least until they are established.

THINNING

Any seedlings of vegetables recently sown *in situ* (eg carrots, spinach, lettuces etc) that are growing strongly should be thinned when they are large enough to handle otherwise they become overcrowded, drawn and weak.

After thinning, always water the rows to settle in the retained plants and get them growing again.

BROAD BEANS

Once the bottom flowers of broad bean plants have formed pods 8–10 cm (3–4 in) long, the tops of the plants should be nipped out to stop them growing any higher than necessary.

This has two effects. First, it channels all the plant's energy into pod and seed formation, which you want to produce a good yield and secondly, it goes a long way towards keeping away pests, particularly the dreaded blackfly.

This is a black aphid which almost invariably infests the growing point of broad beans. If left untreated it will

Spinach beet can be sown this month. It should be picked over regularly to ensure a continuing supply of leaves.

45

seriously weaken the plants. The aphids will usually need spraying with either a systemic insecticide, or one of the insecticides which only kills aphids, so that bees, ladybirds and other beneficial creatures are left unharmed.

WEEDING AND SLUG CONTROL
Keep hoeing amongst all vegetables, especially seedlings and recent transplants. Hoeing not only kills developing weeds, but it also prevents clay soils forming a crust on the surface which can prevent the penetration of air and water.

The final earthing up (see **May, vegetables**) of potatoes this month will also kill any remaining weeds. Its main purpose, though, is to increase the depth of buried stem so that more tubers are encouraged to form.

This is a crucial time for potatoes and they should never be allowed to run short of water once the little tubers are about the size of marbles.

Incidentally, if it is a damp summer

Herbs should be growing well now whether they are in containers or in a herb garden as above. They are most flavoursome when picked young. Chives should have their flowers cut off to encourage new foliage.

there are bound to be underground slugs feeding on the potatoes. They can be kept down by sprinkling slug pellets amongst the rows before you earth them up. Most of the pellets will be buried. Alternatively, water on a liquid metaldehyde slug killer.

WATERING
In the event of a hot, dry summer, watering will be vital. No crop will tolerate a shortage of water and quick growing vegetables, such as early beetroot and carrots, lettuces and cauliflowers, must have abundant moisture to maintain a good rate of growth.

When water is needed, always give plenty so that the equivalent of at least 2·5 cm (1 in) of water is applied. Details of

measuring this are given in **June, lawns**. If these quantities are applied, the vegetables will respond well and there will be no need to water every day. Note that watering a little and often is thoroughly *bad* gardening and will do a great deal more harm than good.

SUPPORTS
Any summer crops in need of support should have been given it before they are in danger of toppling over. Check that all peas, outdoor tomatoes and runner beans have been given all the necessary assistance. Sweet corn may also benefit from either individual canes or a length of twine round the whole block.

HERBS
Mid summer is a good time to cut, dry and preserve herbs. Those that will not dry successfully, such as mint and parsley, will keep beautifully if first frozen and then scrunched up in a polythene bag and put back in the freezer.

RHUBARB

You should stop pulling rhubarb during June so that the plants have time to recover during the rest of the growing season.

You can occasionally ignore the traditional advice that the leaves that are cut off before cooking the stalks must not be composted. This is being over-cautious and normal domestic quantities are perfectly safe. In large amounts rhubarb leaves will create too acidic an environment in the compost heap which will discourage essential micro-organisms.

PEST AND DISEASE CONTROL

Only use chemicals when the need arises.

Aphids of one sort or another are usually bad at this time of year and they may attack almost any crop – broad, French and runner beans, and carrots, are amongst the most susceptible crops.

The cardboard or carpet discs placed around the base of brassica transplants, that have been mentioned in previous months, prevent the female cabbage root fly from laying her eggs at the base of the stem and protect the plants from attack.

FRUIT

June is when the fruit season really begins.

STRAWBERRIES

These are now developing and, in the south of the country, the raspberries will start appearing. Both should be picked over regularly and often. Any that are surplus to your immediate needs can be either frozen, bottled, or made into jam.

A better way of freezing strawberries than as whole, fresh fruits is to use them in cooking a dish and then freeze it. This is a much more satisfactory system. Alternatively, they can be frozen in syrup.

SAFETY CHECK

Although we are normally safe from frosts by June, you should not slacken your vigilance. Even in the south you can get snap frosts early in the month. They are particularly damaging to strawberries and other low growing fruits. Cover the plants with netting or straw in the evening if a frost is suspected, removing the protection early the next morning.

By now you should have stopped de-blossoming perpetual fruiting strawberries, so that future flowers are allowed to develop into fruits. They will be ready after the summer varieties.

Left: Rhubarb has come to the end of its picking season and must build up its strength for next year. Never pull stems the first year after planting.

Below: Rig up a cage of netting over strawberry plants before the fruits begin to ripen, otherwise the crop is likely to be devoured by birds.

BIRD DAMAGE

A fruit cage is certainly the surest and most easily managed method to protect soft fruit from birds but, where this isn't possible, the individual bushes or rows should be netted.

Such methods are the only sure way of protecting the fruit, but good results are sometimes had by treating the ripening fruits with one of the harmless chemical deterrents based on aluminium ammonium sulphate. This should be applied before the birds develop a taste for fruit. Once this has been acquired, it will be very hard to stop them.

Black cotton threaded amongst the branches of bushes, canes and trees is also fairly effective, but not as good as netting. Incidentally, no birds will ever get caught in the cotton, provided it is threaded tight.

CULTIVATION

Once fruits start to develop on any kind of fruit plant, from strawberry to apple tree, watering is essential. If a plant runs short of water, it will start shedding fruit. Although the later stages of development are also important in this respect, it is soon after flowering that the greatest shedding can take place. If a full crop is to be picked, water at the first signs of dryness.

THINNING

If there has been a heavy fruit set of plums, they should be thinned out early in the month and again, if necessary, towards the end. Thinning is normally to 5–8 cm (2–3 in), but large varieties like 'Victoria' and 'Pond's' should be to the wider spacing of 8–10 cm (3–4 in).

Peach fruitlets should be thinned and singled to about 15 cm (6 in) apart and new shoots wanted for extension growths tied in regularly.

If dessert gooseberries were not thinned last month and are in need of it, thin them

THINNING PEACHES

BEFORE

AFTER

Peach fruitlets should be reduced to one per cluster and further thinned so that each fruit is about 15 cm (6 in) apart. This will ensure good quality fruits of reasonable size are formed.

now and use the thinnings for cooking. The first thinning should involve removing alternate berries and, if crowding is still apparent later in the month, remove those causing it. Apples and pears are not normally thinned until next month.

Also, as the new canes of blackberry and hybrid cane fruits grow and develop, tie them in so that they are neither damaged nor cause overcrowding.

STRAWBERRY SLUG CONTROL

Strawberries will be growing well by now, so the ground beneath them should be covered with straw, or one of the substitutes available, to prevent the berries resting on the soil and becoming mud

Left: June is the month for summer pruning cordon-trained gooseberries. This method of training is quite simple and will make gathering the berries less painful.

Left: *Paeonia lactiflora* hybrids are available in white and shades of red, pink and peach with double or single flowers. Give the plants a well drained and fertile soil and leave them undisturbed for best results.

Below: Hostas flower in June but are valued most for their foliage. Like all hostas, *H. undulata* enjoys moisture and dappled shade.

splashed and eaten by slugs.

Straw is normally only readily available in country areas, but there are several alternatives that will do the job. Probably the most convenient are the bitumenized paper mats. They tend to be slightly too small for second- and third-year plants, but are admirable for first years. Slitted or perforated black polythene sheeting is better because the ground around and between the plants can be covered. It will just need to be weighted to the ground with stones to stop it blowing away. Avoid using ordinary unslitted polythene. It collects the rain and, frequently, the berries lie in puddles.

PRUNING

Gooseberries and red currants may be summer pruned towards the end of June. While this is by no means essential with traditionally shaped bushes, it has definite benefits with cordons. In its simplest form,

summer pruning consists of cutting back all new side shoots, not the extension growth on the end of each branch, to 10–13 cm (4–5 in) long.

PEST CONTROL

Good control of pests and diseases earlier in the year will have reduced their numbers or even overcome them. They should never be ignored, though. Especially as now, in June, comes the codling moth.

It is responsible for the maggots that we often find in apples, and sometimes pears, after they have been picked. The caterpillars enter the developing fruits during June, so effective action must be taken now or else it will be too late.

Spray with an insecticide containing the chemical permethrin in the middle of the month, and again at the end or in early July. Both are necessary to take account of the period over which the eggs are laid and hatch out.

JULY

FLOWERS AND SHRUBS

Deadheading should continue whenever and wherever it is needed, not only on roses. Other flowers that need it are herbaceous plants and, in particular, bedding plants. A good display of flowers will only be had right through the summer and into the autumn if the old flowerheads are removed and the plant is therefore prevented from setting seed. Look out for rose suckers and deal with them as described in **June, flowers and shrubs.**

SEEDLINGS AND YOUNG PLANTS

Any herbaceous and biennial seedlings that are still in their original seed rows, or pots, should be planted out in wider nursery rows soon after they are large enough to handle. Any that were planted some time ago and which are now needing more space can, if the room is available, be planted out where they are to flower.

Also, sow any herbaceous plant seeds still remaining. There is still time to build good plants by the winter, but they are very unlikely to flower until next year.

CONTAINERS

If you grow plants in window boxes, hanging baskets, tubs, or any other similar container, make sure that they are well looked after. Once in flower and growing well, they will need liquid feeding at least weekly. Watering will be more frequent and should usually be given when the surface of the compost is drying out. Deadheading is another job that must not be neglected.

PRUNING

Most shrubs that flower from about now onwards do so on the growth that they have made this season. These should not be pruned until late winter or early spring. The two exceptions are wisteria and rambler roses. New and long wisteria shoots that are not wanted for tying in to increase the size of the plant should be cut back to 15 cm (6 in) long now, and in the winter to two buds to encourage flowering. Rambler roses need to be pruned to help enlarge and ripen next summer's flowering shoots.

DISBUDDING

Early flowering chrysanthemums may need disbudding if they are grown as single flowers, rather than as sprays.

PLANTS FOR JULY

Deciduous trees and shrubs
Catalpa
Ceanothus 'Gloire de Versailles'
Cytisus battandieri
Fuchsia (many cultivars)
Genista
Hydrangea
Hypericum
Liriodendron tulipifera
Philadelphus (mock orange, syringa)
Potentilla (shrubby)
Roses
Spartium junceum (broom)
Spiraea
Tamarix ramosissima

Evergreen trees and shrubs
Calluna vulgaris (ling, many cultivars)
Carpenteria
Cistus
Erica cinerea (many cultivars)
Escallonia
Hebe
Hypericum calycinum (rose of Sharon)
Lavandula (lavender)
Olearia haastii
Phlomis fruticosa (Jerusalem sage)
Senecio 'Sunshine'
Vinca
Yucca

Climbers
Clematis
Jasminum officinale
Lathyrus latifolius (perennial pea)
Lonicera (honeysuckle)
Passiflora (passion flower)
Roses (climbing)
Solanum crispum

Bulbs
Allium
Cardiocrinum
Crocosmia
Gladiolus
Lilium
Tigridia

Herbaceous perennials
Achillea
Agapanthus
Alstromeria
Aruncus
Astilbe
Astrantia
Campanula (bell flowers)
Chrysanthemum maximum (Shasta daisy)
Clematis integrifolia
Delphinium
Dianthus
Echinops (globe thistle)
Erigeron
Eryngium
Gaillardia
Geranium (hardy)
Geum
Helenium
Heliopsis
Hemerocallis (day lily)
Hosta (plantain lily)
Inula
Kniphofia (red hot poker)
Lavatera olbia (mallow)
Lysimachia
Monarda
Nepeata
Oenothera (evening primrose)
Penstemon
Phlox
Polygonum (knotweed)
Romneya
Verbascum (mullein)

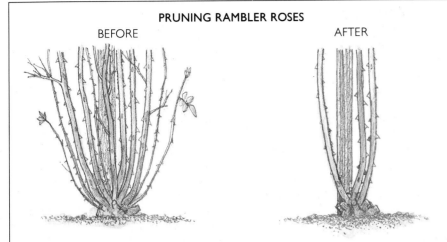

PRUNING RAMBLER ROSES

BEFORE

AFTER

Ramblers, unlike other roses, should be pruned in summer. Untie stems and cut out all those that have borne flowers.

The young stems that remain should be tied in to their supports. They will now mature and may flower next year.

When the initial four or so side shoots have developed, you will see that buds in the leaf axils will then start to grow out.

With single flowered varieties, all these embryonic shoots and flower buds must be removed so that only the central flower-bud at the end of the main 'branches' is allowed to remain and develop.

WATERING

Although there never seems to be as much need to water flowers and shrubs as there does vegetables and lawns, it should never be neglected. Always apply a sufficient quantity to soak well down into the soil, as wetting the surface is worse than useless because this encourages new roots to form in the upper soil where water is always less plentiful.

WEEDS AND PEST CONTROL

Weeds must also continue to be kept down by hoe or by hand.

Along with weed control goes pest and disease control. Black spot and mildew may be seen on roses while greenfly attacks a wide range of plants.

FINAL CONSIDERATIONS

If beech and hornbeam hedges are clipped late in July, their leaves will still turn brown in the autumn but will stay on

during the winter, so providing a similar amount of shelter to an evergreen hedge.

Propagate hydrangeas from cuttings before the end of the month. After then, many will have formed flower buds in the tops and will be unsuitable.

LAWNS

Even in a damp summer, lawns will tend to slow down their growth rate after peaking in June. However, you should never neglect mowing. In a dry summer leave the grass-box off the mower once or twice to allow the mowings to fly. This will help to keep the grass in good condition by providing a very shallow mulch. The height of the cut should also be raised by about 1 cm ($\frac{1}{2}$ in).

LAWN TONIC

All lawns appreciate a summer tonic to buck them up and keep them going for the rest of the growing season. If you are not able or prepared to water the lawn after using a granular feed, you should feed only before rain is forecast. Alternatively, apply one of the several liquid feeds specially formulated for lawns.

If the lawn is in need of watering, revealed by the lack of growth and the possible appearance of dry and even brown patches, carry it out as described in **June, lawns.**

This mixed bed includes *Papaver somniferum, Layia, Agrostemma, Malope* and *Malcomia.*

51

Plant up hanging baskets and window boxes generously for best effect. Then, to keep them looking good, feed plants regularly, water frequently and cut off any faded blooms throughout the summer.

WEEDING

Weedkilling can still be carried out very effectively, but it should only be done when the grass and weeds are growing well. A feed and thorough watering about one week before you plan to use a lawn weedkiller is particularly beneficial. Unless, of course, you plan to use a combined material, in which case omit the feed and just apply the water.

ANTS

Ants can be a nuisance in lawns after mid summer. They don't eat the grass, but they hide it beneath their nests which can pile up to 10 cm (4 in) or so. This not only looks awful, but makes mowing quite a problem, and creates seedbeds for weeds and moss. Brush the anthill out of the way so that it is scattered over the lawn, and then treat the nest with a proprietary ant or lawn pest killer as instructed by the manufacturer, or pour boiling water into it.

LAWN DISEASE

Something that puzzles many gardeners towards the end of the summer is the appearance of small brown patches in the lawn, which may increase in size and even join up. Close examination will usually reveal that amongst the brown blades of grass there are what look like thin pink blades as well. These are the fungal bodies of the red thread (corticium) disease. The main cause of corticium is undernourished grass, so feeding is the obvious prevention. However, the disease must be killed and, fortunately, a general fungicide containing benomyl is very effective.

VEGETABLES

Last month we mentioned preserving herbs by one means or another. This still holds good for July, but it should not be left too late or they will be past their best.

WATERING

We also saw last month that many vegetables need to be kept growing without check from drought if they are to be at their best. Salad crops such as lettuces and radishes are obvious examples, but cauliflowers are another. They must be grown quickly if they are to attain a curd of good size. Full details of watering are given in **June, lawns**.

Above: *Hemerocallis* has a long flowering season despite the fact that each flower only lasts a day — hence their familiar name of day lily. This clump-forming perennial can be divided in autumn or spring.

Left: Tuberous begonias are ideal plants for bedding or for growing in containers where their magnificent flowers can be appreciated. Lift and store tubers in peat over winter.

HOLIDAY ACTION

One of the main jobs for many people this month is preparing for a holiday. You should therefore make sure that all the vegetables which are ready, or nearly so, are picked and dealt with before you go.

As regards those that mature while you are away, the best thing is to ask a neighbour to gather them in.

Before your departure you should give your crops an application of top-dressing and fertilizer. Follow this up with a heavy watering. Also look out for signs of pests or diseases (eg caterpillars on brassicas) and tackle them before you go. Any that are left there when you go will have a field day in your absence.

If you have any frames or cloches covering crops, remove them before you depart to avoid the risk of over-heating or shortage of water. Any seedlings or young plants that need planting out should either be dealt with at least one week before you go, and then watered freely to get them established quickly, or left in their nursery rows until you get back.

Finally, if your runner beans have reached the top of their canes, nip out the tops to encourage pod formation and growth. At the same time it will lead to the development of stronger side shoots and, consequently, more beans.

COMPOSTING
All waste vegetables and spent plants can go on the heap or into the bin. For the best and quickest composting, add a proprietary compost activator to the raw material every 15 cm (6 in) or so, as the heap or bin builds up.

Never add layers of soil to compost heaps or bins as so often recommended. They create cold layers within the heap and result in uneven composting.

Compost started at this time of year will normally be fit for use by the autumn because of the relatively warm conditions.

THINNING AND PLANTING
Look out for seedlings that need to be thinned and don't let them get too big. The most likely candidates are to be found amongst lettuces, carrots, swedes, beetroot and turnips, sown last month.

Any brassica seedlings still in their seed beds will need to be planted out in their final position early in the month if they are to make good plants before the autumn. On average set them 45 cm (18 in) apart, though as mentioned last month, spring cabbages should go in at half that distance so that every other plant can be used in the spring for an early picking.

Suitable varieties (see **May, vegetables**) of turnips, beetroot and carrots, can all be sown early in the month, as can winter radishes (red or black skinned) and lettuces for autumn use.

PESTS AND DISEASES
There are no specially bad pests or diseases restricted to July. The normal nasties, such as greenfly and cabbage root fly on brassicas, will have to be guarded against, along with carrot fly after a row has just been thinned. Watering the carrot seedlings straight after thinning gives added protection by quickly reviving any that are flagging and reducing their attractive scent.

Potato blight In a wet summer, potato blight may be seen on the leaves of potato plants as yellow and then brown patches, accompanied by a fungus. Copper sprays will usually clear up the disease but a product containing mancozeb is even better. Always spray at the first sign of trouble or the disease will usually spread down into the developing tubers. This makes them inedible, and later rotten. Even worse, the disease will linger on to the following year.

Left: Red hot poker, *Kniphofia galpinii* grows to 60 cm (2 ft). It thrives in well drained, even poor soil and flowers well into the autumn.

Above: *Agapanthus* 'Headbourne Hybrids' is an outstanding African lily. It needs a full sun, a moist soil and should be divided in the spring.

Left: Ripe strawberries must be picked over daily. When the whole crop has finished, remove old foliage, stalks and runners that have grown.

Above: Pick peas while they are young and sweet. If left too long on the plant they will lose their flavour. It is a good idea to net plants against birds.

FRUIT

Now we really are getting into the fruit season. All fruits that are ready should be picked without delay to stop them spoiling on the plant.

FRUITS IN SEASON

The main fruits now maturing are strawberries, raspberries, currants (black, red and white), gooseberries, cherries, and peaches. Also, possibly the very earliest of the plums, such as 'Czar', though early August is more usual.

TYING IN

If necessary check and replace all ties holding in trained trees or bushes. If any haven't been loosened over the past months they could well be biting into the bark by now, as the girth of the trunk or branch increases. As a branch's expansion is restricted by a tie, the supply of sap will be reduced or even stopped.

Any new shoots (both main and lateral) of trained trees that have not been tied in should be done so soon, because the wood will start to harden up and become inflexible, making it difficult to train the shoots in the required direction.

THINNING APPLES

If there is an exceptionally heavy crop of apples, or if a biennial variety such as 'Laxton's Superb' is fruiting, thinning the crop is probably advisable. If an abundance of young apples is not thinned, they will not grow very large.

Most varieties will naturally shed fruitlets during the summer and, although this is officially termed 'the June drop', nine years out of ten it occurs in early July. Any manual thinning should be left until after this natural thinning has finished. As a general rule, eating apples should be thinned to 10–15 cm (4–6 in) and cooking varieties to 15–23 cm (6–9 in).

It is normal to thin to one fruit per cluster, but this is not a golden rule and it can be varied. You should start by removing any diseased, damaged or mis-shapen fruits. The next to go, if necessary, are the 'king' fruits, those growing with a short, fat stalk and in the centre of the cluster. After that, it is largely a matter of what size you prefer; the more you thin, the larger the remaining fruits.

SUPPORT AND WATERING

Any branches of any tree which are showing signs of being weighed down by fruit to a dangerous extent should be supported. One way is to place a tall pole by the tree, with lead strings down to the branches taking the weight off them; another is to support the branches with short props of wood or metal rods. Plum trees especially, can be heavily laden now.

Make sure that no fruits are allowed to go short of water during this critical time.

AFTER FRUITING
As soon as summer raspberries, loganberries, tayberries and any other cane fruits have finished fruiting, the old canes should be cut away at ground level and the new canes tied in place.

Summer strawberries If they have been cropping for three seasons, most varieties should be replaced with new plants. However, if plants are being kept for a second or third year, cut off the foliage and old fruit stalks along with any runners that have developed with a pair of shears, but avoid cutting into the crown of the plant. This treatment encourages

PRUNING SUMMER RASPBERRIES

Cut out old fruited canes and any that are weak and spindly, or growing some distance from the row. Tie new canes to training wires so they are spaced about 10 cm (4 in) apart.

Terra-cotta pots and containers full of flowering annuals such as petunias (here growing with variegated ivy) enliven any part of the garden. Stand them on the patio or use them to mark the transition from one area of the garden to another. This could be a change of level or a change of style (for instance from lawn to kitchen garden).

'Czar' is an early ripening plum which may be ready for picking at the end of July. Plum trees can be heavily laden in some years and their brittle wood may crack under the weight unless support is given. Such damage not only results in a reduced yield but provides an entry point for diseases.

strong new leaves to grow and fruit buds to establish within the plants. It will also remove a lot of pests and diseases. All the debris, along with any straw, can be composted. The plants are then given a top-dressing of Growmore at a rate of 64 g per m² (2 oz per sq yd).

APPLE AND PEAR CORDONS

Cordons or espaliers will benefit enormously from summer pruning late in the month. Only shoots of the current season's growth, and which have hardened at the base and are approaching pencil thickness are involved. Those that are growing directly from a main branch or stem are cut back to about 8 cm (3 in) long to a bud. Those which are growing from a previously pruned shoot or spur go back to 3 cm (1 in). Those shoots which have not attained the correct state of maturity are left until September.

The only shoots to leave unpruned (besides the immature ones) are those which are wanted for extension growth on the end of the main branches or the central stem (leader).

PESTS AND DISEASES

The same comments apply as to **June, fruit**. In addition, though, red spider mites could be troublesome on apples, particularly if the weather is dry, and will need a systemic insecticide to kill them. Also, remember the second spray against codling moth on apples, if it has not already been applied – again, see **June**.

TRAINING CANE FRUITS

6½ ft
5 ft
4 ft
3½ ft

2 m
1·5 m
1·2 m
1 m

Fruiting canes should be looped and tied to the lower wires. Cut these out after fruiting and tie in the new canes that have been trained up the centre.

AUGUST

FLOWERS AND SHRUBS

You will probably be getting extremely bored by being told so regularly to keep weeds under control! But if you don't and let them flower, they will soon drop their seeds over a huge area. They will then lie dormant over the winter. Any digging on your part will only disperse them even further, and next spring they will take over as they burst forth.

Don't forget, too, that flower borders still need to be watered (see **June, flowers and shrubs**), and that flowers must be regularly deadheaded.

COLLECTING SEEDS

Now that the growing season is drawing to a close you may want to save seeds from certain plants for sowing next year.

These plants should, of course, be al-
lowed to form seedheads naturally. When they are starting to open, but before the seeds are released, pick off the heads and keep them in a paper bag to dry.

Once the heads are opening, the bags can be shaken to release the seeds. As soon as you have a good quantity, pour the seeds into a small airtight bottle, or similar container, label and store them in a cool room or in the attic (not a fridge) until the sowing time. Kept like this, they should remain healthy for several years.

SOWING

However, some hardy annuals can be sown now in their flowering positions, so that they spend the winter outdoors. They will make far better plants and flower much earlier next summer. Those seeds suitable include: English marigold (*Calen-*
dula), Californian poppy (*Eschscholtzia*), godetia, gypsophila, evening primrose (*Oenothera*), soapwort (*Saponaria*), sweet peas, and catchfly (*Silene*).

Bulbs

You should plant autumn flowering bulbs early in the month, the most popular and widely grown being the autumn crocus. In fact, this is not a true crocus but belongs to the genus *Colchicum*, though its flower is very crocus-like. Plant now so that the tops are about 5 cm (2 in) underground. It will start growing immediately and will be in flower during September.

PROPAGATING SHRUBS

This is the time of year to propagate almost all hardy shrubs. It is by no means essential to have a greenhouse for this

---

PLANTS FOR AUGUST

Deciduous trees and shrubs

Abelia
Buddleia davidii vars.
Ceanothus 'Gloire de Versailles'
Clerodendrum
Fuchsia (many cultivars)
Hydrangea (many cultivars)
Hypericum
Leycesteria formosa
Perovskia
Potentilla (shrubby)
Roses
Spartium junceum (broom)

Evergreen trees and shrubs

Calluna vulgaris (ling, many cultivars)
Carpenteria
Cistus

Erica cinerea (many cultivars)
Escallonia
Hebe
Hypericum calycinum (rose of Sharon)
Lavendula (lavender)
Olearia × *haastii*
Phlomis fruticosa (Jerusalem sage)
Senecio 'Sunshine'
Vinca (periwinkle)
Yucca

Climbers

Bilderdykia (*Polygonum*) *baldschuanicum*
Clematis (large-flowered)
Jasminum officinale
Lonicera (honeysuckle)
Passiflora (passion flower)
Roses (climbing)

Solanum
Tropaeolum

Bulbs

Amaryllis
Crocosmia
Dahlia (many cultivars)
Gladiolus
Lilium (lily)
Montbretia
Tigridia

Herbaceous perennials

Acanthus
Achillea
Althaea (hollyhock)
Alstromeria
Anemone japonica (many cultivars)
Aster
Astilbe
Campanula (bellflowers)
Chrysanthemum
Echinops (globe thistle)

Gypsophila
Helenium
Helianthus
Heliopsis
Hemerocallis (day lily)
Hosta (plantain lily)
Inula
Kniphofia (red hot poker)
Lysimachia
Monarda (bee balm)
Nepeta (cat nip)
Oenothera (evening primrose)
Penstemon
Phlox
Polygonum (knotweed)
Romneya
Rudbeckia
Salvia superba
Sedum
Solidago (golden rod)
Tradescantia virginiana (spiderwort)

TAKING CUTTINGS

The finished cutting should be no more than 15 cm (6 in) long. Dip the base in rooting powder and tap off any excess.

With a razor blade or a very sharp knife trim the cutting to just below a leaf joint. Remove the lower leaves to give 2 or 3 cm (about 1 in) of clear stem.

Insert the cuttings round the edge of a pot filled with a seed or cutting compost. Water in and place the pot inside a polythene bag or propagator.

purpose, but it helps a great deal as the warmer conditions lead to quicker rooting.

Even without a greenhouse, though, you can get perfectly acceptable results by using a cloche or frame outside, made airtight with a covering of polythene. A windowsill is also a good place, but avoid one that is in direct sun for long periods.

Take cuttings of this year's growth – sturdy, quite short, and nearly always from the outside of the bush where they have been ripened by the sun.

RAMBLERS AND CLIMBERS
Finish pruning rambler roses as soon as you can so that the new shoots have time to harden up and ripen in what is left of the summer. This will make them flower much better next year.

As described last month, all the shoots that have finished flowering should be cut right out at ground level. After pruning, tie in the new shoots to take their place.

Many climbing plants (such as the early-flowering clematis and wisteria) will have been growing furiously during the summer and could now be in need of attention. Tie them in loosely now, so that the new growth is not blown about and damaged.

PEST CONTROL
Most pests and diseases should have been controlled by now, but fungi such as rose black spot and mildew will still need treatment to avoid the production and spread of overwintering spores. If left, they will spread the diseases next year.

LAWNS
The final summer feed of the year should be given during the second half of the month. This will have a high nitrogen content to encourage growth.

If the disease corticium (see **June, lawns**) has been troublesome, this last feed will help the lawn to recover and will

also help to discourage the fungus.

NEW LAWNS FROM SEED
Final preparations (including raking and any shallow levelling) should be under way. Avoid deep digging or the soil will not have enough time to settle before sowing. If any weeds are present on the area, hoe them off shallowly. If they are

Echinops ritro, the globe thistle, has deeply cut grey-green foliage. This sun-loving perennial grows to 1 m (3 ft) and is very attractive to bees.

Left: Runner beans will need to be picked over every day or two at this time of the year.

Above: Courgettes will also need to be picked before they get too large if a plentiful supply of tender young fruits is to be maintained.

allowed to remain, they stand a very good chance of smothering the new grass.

Rake the surface as fine as you can and remove stones. Immediately before this final raking, apply a pre-sowing feed together with, if necessary, some fine grade peat or bark to improve the quality of the soil. The feed will sustain the seedlings once they appear.

If your preparations have not reached this advanced stage, it would be better on all but the sandiest of soils to delay sowing until next month, or even the spring.

Sowing Provided that the weather is not too hot and dry, and that the soil is in a fit condition, new lawns should be sown towards the end of the month or early in September. Choose a day that is not too windy, so that the seed does not blow away, and carry out the job as follows.

First, the area is marked out in strips 1 m (3½ ft) wide. The type of seed mix to buy will depend on the kind of lawn you require. If it's going to get heavy wear, you need a lot of ryegrass in the mix.

Calculate the amount of seed needed for each strip on the basis of 48 g per m² (1·5 oz per sq yd) and put the right amount in a tin or jar at the end of each strip.

Sprinkle the seed evenly over each strip until the whole lawn is sown. The marking string, canes, etc, are then removed and the seed is raked in lightly. If the soil is dry and rain is not expected, water the area thoroughly, but gently, so that the surface is not puddled and beaten down

Aftercare Keeping cats and birds off the sown area is achieved either by netting the lawn or laying twiggy sticks on it. Alternatively, water on a harmless chemical deterrent, such as those based on aluminium ammonium sulphate. Signs of germination should be seen in one to two weeks, according to the temperature. The new lawn will thus be well established before the winter.

WEED CONTROL

Good control of lawn weeds is still possible during August, but it is unwise to leave it much later.

VEGETABLES

Gather all vegetables as they ripen. Crops such as peas, beans and courgettes must be gathered regularly and frequently. They are at their best when young and tender, and the plants will stop cropping if too many 'fruits' are allowed to mature. It is much better to give away any surplus than to leave it on the plant.

If you are going away on holiday this month, follow the procedure recommended in July, and make arrangements for a neighbour to look after the vegetables by picking any that are ready.

WATERING

Root vegetables in particular should be kept well watered during any dry spells

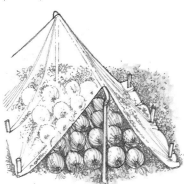

A week or so later pull up the bulbs and lay them on the ground to ripen, preferably under a polythene tent to keep off any rain.

Once the tops of onions and shallots show signs of falling over lift the bulbs slightly so the roots are severed but the bulbs remain in the ground.

otherwise they will stop growing. Even worse, when the rains do come there will be a sudden surge of growth that will cause them to split.

Recently transplanted cabbages and other brassicas are especially susceptible to drying out. Watering with a sprinkler is usually unnecessary as a watering can is perfectly adequate.

Rows of seedlings are also likely to dry out quite quickly, and should also be watered with a can.

PLANTING OUT AND SOWING

Plant out any brassicas still in their seed rows. They are most likely to be cabbages and cauliflowers, which should now be planted 45–60 cm (18–24 in) apart.

Sow spring cabbages 1 cm ($\frac{1}{2}$ in) deep in nursery rows, and spring onions 1 cm ($\frac{1}{2}$ in) deep in rows 10 cm (4 in) apart. Keep them well watered after sowing so that the seeds germinate quickly and the plants grow quickly. Also, lettuces (eg 'Dandie' or 'Kwiek') may be sown in frames for autumn use.

Any remaining rows of carrot, turnip or swede seedlings that are to be thinned and singled should be attended to when they are large enough to handle. Also, always water a row immediately after thinning so that the retained seedlings grow away quickly and strongly.

TOMATOES

As soon as single stemmed outdoor tomatoes (not bush varieties) have formed four strong trusses of flowers, the top should be nipped out of the plant to leave just two leaves above the top truss.

This will channel all the plant's energy into fruit production and ensure that all the tomatoes left on the plant stand a good chance of ripening, or at least of growing to a good size.

Developing root crops such as carrots (left) and beetroot (right) will need watering during dry spells. Aim to keep the ground evenly moist throughout the growing season. This will help produce good quality vegetables of superior flavour.

ONIONS

Onions have always been a popular garden vegetable, and in August you must prepare to harvest and dry them off (see illustration).

When the onion tops and roots are completely dry, which will take another two to three weeks, they are fit for storing. This is most conveniently done by keeping them in net bags that you see in most greengrocers. They should then be stored in a dry and frost-free shed or garage.

PESTS AND DISEASES

With the reduction in sunshine and daylight hours, fungus diseases often build up at this time of year. Be on the look-out for trouble of this sort, and treat any plants appropriately that are showing symptoms. Potato blight is a case in point, but there are several others to avoid.

Cabbage white caterpillars can, if you feel inclined, be picked off by hand. Aphids too are likely to be seen on many plants, especially the mealy cabbage aphid on brassicas. Use either a systemic insecticide or one specific to aphids that will leave beneficial insects unharmed.

FRUIT

August is probably the richest month of the year for the variety of fruits available.

Shasta daisy, or *Chrysanthemum maximum*, provides a good supply of cut flowers throughout the summer. It needs a well drained, quite rich soil and a sunny position.

FRUITS IN SEASON

These include apples, pears, plums, maybe some late cherries, peaches, nectarines, strawberries, raspberries, currants, gooseberries, blackberries, and loganberries, plus other hybrid berries will probably be ready during the month.

At this time of year it is best to allow all fruits, except pears, to ripen on the plant. Gather them, therefore, when they are ready and, as with vegetables, never leave them in the hope that they will improve – most will deteriorate. Pears should be picked just before they are ripe, and when they part quite easily from the tree – ripen them indoors.

SUPPORT

Any branches heavily laden with fruit will need supporting if they are not to be broken. Plums are particularly likely to suffer from this because of their rather brittle wood and the habit of producing either very light or very heavy crops. The various methods of support are described in **July, fruit**.

PROTECTION AND PRUNING

Ripening fruit is a particularly favourite food of blackbirds and starlings. Soft fruit (raspberries, strawberries, currants, etc) are best protected by either a fruit cage or by covering the bushes or rows with netting. Trees trained to walls, fences or wires may also be netted, as can small free-standing trees.

Large trees, however, are far less easy to protect, and one usually has to resort to hanging things on the branches that glitter and make a noise. These are seldom very effective though.

Trained apples and pears Summer pruning (see **July, fruit**) can be carried out early in the month in the north of the country. This will channel more energy into the developing fruits, at the same time as they are being ripened by the sun. The wood, too, will mature, thus strengthening the fruit buds which have recently formed for next year.

Plums These normally need very little pruning beyond correcting overcrowded branches and removing any that are dead, damaged or diseased. A good habit to acquire involves doing any necessary

TRAINED APPLES AND PEARS

Cut back the current season's new growth to 8 cm (3 in), just above a bud. Shoots needed for extension growth should not be pruned.

pruning on plums straight after they have fruited. This goes a long way towards protecting the trees from infection by the silver leaf fungus.

Once silver leaf is in a tree, it often proves fatal. Its symptoms are evident when leaves, on one or more branches, develop a silvery sheen during the growing season. Control is sometimes possible by removing the infected branches.

The disease is at its most infectious during the winter, when the spores are liberated. Any large cut in the tree that they land on will provide an entry point, whereas by pruning after fruiting, any wounds will become sealed (though not completely healed) before the winter.

Peaches (and nectarines) These are also pruned now, or in September, after

fruiting. Pruning now strengthens the shoots and next year's fruit buds. Because peaches fruit only on the shoots that grew in the previous season, any that have carried fruit are no longer required. They are therefore cut back hard to a replacement shoot which will have grown out from near the base during the year. This will carry fruit in the following year and should be tied in to the supporting wires on the wall or fence.

A free-standing peach tree (untrained) need not be pruned with the same precision as an espalier or fan. In fact, the same method that has just been described for plums suits them well.

Summer fruiting raspberries Those which have finished fruiting, but which have not been pruned yet, should be

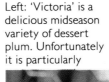

Left: 'Victoria' is a delicious midseason variety of dessert plum. Unfortunately it is particularly susceptible to silver leaf disease.

Below: Red currant 'Red Lake' can be relied upon to produce a good crop.

attended to without delay. Cut out the fruited canes right down to the ground and tie in the new ones to replace them. They should be approximately 10 cm (4 in) apart along the top wire after tying in.

Autumn fruiting raspberries Run a supporting twine down each side of the rows, secured to a post at each end.

Blackberries and hybrid cane fruits When they have finished cropping, the fruited canes should be cut down to the ground and the new canes trained in to take their place. However, some blackberries, ie 'Himalaya Giant', produce very few new canes each year, sometimes just one. If this happens, it is quite permissible to shorten some of the fruited canes' strong side shoots.

STRAWBERRIES
Probably the most important job amongst the soft fruits involves planting new strawberries. They should be in by the middle of the month if you are to pick the maximum potential crop next summer.

Although you can quite easily grow new plants from the runners produced by established strawberries, it is better to buy in certified plants. They will be guaranteed completely free of virus diseases, which is more than can be said of many of those raised at home.

Varieties Some gardeners still hanker after 'Royal Sovereign'. However, it has now been superseded by far better modern varieties. Another old favourite is 'Cambridge Vigour', which has been the standard early variety for many years, especi-

ally for growing under cloches and in greenhouses. An even earlier favourite is 'Pantagruella' – not such a good all-rounder, and a smaller plant. 'Cambridge Favourite' has long been the mainstay of both the fruit industry (as it looks good and travels well) and gardeners.

However, the new Dutch variety 'Elsanta' is fast overtaking 'Cambridge Favourite'; it is much better, has excellent flavour, large berries, and heavy crops. The latest summer variety is the excellent, new 'Malling Pandora'. It fruits from mid July to mid August in the south, by which time the perpetual (autumn fruiting) varities have begun, thus ensuring an unbroken supply of fresh strawberries from June well into October. All these summer varieties should be planted 40 cm (16 in) apart in rows 45 cm (18 in) apart.

Left: Blackberries will be fruiting now on canes produced last year. They are vigorous growers so leave at least 3 m (10 ft) between plants. In most gardens they are best trained along a boundary fence.

Below: The loganberry season will be coming to an end and fruited canes should be cut out. Like most hybrid cane fruits, loganberries are the result of a raspberry/blackberry cross.

SEPTEMBER

FLOWERS AND SHRUBS

In the world of bulbs, corms and tubers, September is a very important month. It is the time for attending to those which have just flowered, and planting spring flowering subjects outdoors, along with those which are to flower indoors in bowls during the winter.

Except in the milder parts of the country, it really isn't safe to leave half-hardy bulbs in the ground during the winter. If they are not killed by the weather, then slugs or mice will probably get them.

LIFTING AND STORING GLADIOLI AND DAHLIAS

These are obvious candidates for transferral, as are freesias. When their foliage has half-yellowed, dig them up carefully, label them (variety and description), and cut the tops back to about 1 in (2·5 cm). Some people leave the tops on to die down completely, but this is inviting diseases.

Dry corms under cover, clean them by removing the old roots and any bulbils (which can be grown on) and store them in a frost-free place until the spring.

OUTDOOR BULBS

Although certain bulbs for flowering outdoors next spring can be planted from now until as late as November, for the sake of completeness we will look at the subject now. There are many ways and places that we can grow bulbs outdoors.

Formal bedding   This is certainly the most spectacular, but by no means all bulbs are suitable. For example, daffodils and other narcissi have far too much foliage, and are over well before it is time to plant the summer bedding.

Pride of place for a low-growing display must go to the hyacinths. They are perfect for growing in tubs or window boxes.

Many of the early flowering tulips are also excellent, but it is the May flowering tulips that steal the show. There are so many to choose from, Darwins, paeony-flowered, triumph, lily-flowered, Rembrandt, and parrot being the main ones. One of the best ways of growing them is amongst other spring flowering bedding plants, such as wallflowers.

Even people without a garden can grow bulbs in tubs, troughs, window boxes or hanging baskets.

Naturalizing bulbs   The opposite to formal bedding is 'naturalizing'. This is where the daffodils and narcissi really come into their own. In addition, you could have aconites, snowdrops and snowflakes (leucojum), crocuses (for a sunny position) and a host of others. Always grow naturalized bulbs in bold groups so that they really make an impact.

Rock gardens are another place where small bulbs can be naturalized. The following are just a few of the more popular rock garden bulbs: aconites, anemone, chionodoxa, crocus, cyclamen, miniature

---

PLANTS FOR SEPTEMBER

Deciduous trees and shrubs
Abelia
Buddleia davidii (butterfly bush)
Ceanothus
Cotinus coggygria and 'Folis Purpureis'
Fuchsia
Hibiscus syriacus
Hydrangea
Hypericum
Leycesteria formosa
Perovskia
Potentilla (shrubby)
Roses
Spartinium junceum (broom)
Tamarix ramosissima

Evergreen shrubs
Abelia grandiflora
Hebe
Hypericum calycinum
Vinca (periwinckle)
Yucca

Climbers
Bilderdykia (Polygonum) baldschuanicum
Clematis orientalis
Clematis tangutica
Rosa bracteata
Solanum crispum 'Autumnale'

Bulbs
Amaryllis
Colchicum

Crocosmia
Crocus (autumn)
Cyclamen neapolitanum
Dahlias
Leucojum autumnale
Lilium auratum
Lilium speciosum
Nerine bowdenii

Herbaceous perennials
Acanthus (bear's breeches)
Achillea ptarmica
Althaea (hollyhock)
Alstromeria
Anemone × hybrida (many cultivars)
Aster (Michaelmas daisies)

Astilbe
Chrysanthemum
Gaillardia
Helenium
Helianthus
Heliopsis
Hemerocallis (day lily)
Kniphofia (red hot poker)
Liriope muscari
Oenothera (evening primrose)
Romneya
Rudbeckia
Salvia superba
Schizostylis
Sedum
Solidago (golden rod)

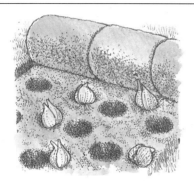

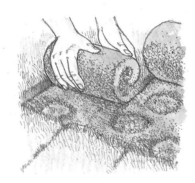

When planting large groups of bulbs in grass, skim back the turf and plant them in the exposed soil.

After planting roll the turf back in place and firm it down.

Use a special bulb planter or trowel to lift a core of turf and soil. The bulb is dropped in. Replace the core after removing the lowest portion.

Left: Rose of Sharon, *Hypericum calycinum*, is a tough ground covering shrub for a dry bank or a spot where little else will grow. A clip over after flowering is the only pruning necessary.

iris species, miniature narcissi and grape hyacinths – the choice is endless.

Most of us, though, will end up planting our bulbs in mixed borders. Soil preparations are minimal, but do note that no bulb likes growing in wet ground so the drainage must be good. This can always be improved by putting some coarse sand in the holes before planting the bulb. After planting bulbs in a mixed border or in grass, always mark their position with sticks so that you don't dig them up or mow over them later on.

PLANTING GUIDE TO BULBS

Although the depth at which bulbs are planted is not critical, there are guidelines that should be observed for the best results. The following depths are taken from the base of the bulb – in other words, the depth of the hole in which the bulb is planted. A useful aid to planting bulbs is a special bulb trowel with the depth marked off from the point.

Bulb	Depth of hole	Distance
Anemone	8 cm	10–15 cm
	(3 in)	(4–6 in)
Crocus	5 cm	5 cm
	(2 in)	(2 in)
Daffodils	18 cm	30 cm
(*Narcissus*)	(7 in)	(1 ft)
Daffodils – miniature	7.5–10 cm	10–30 cm
(*Narcissus*)	(3–4 in)	(4 in–1 ft)
Hyacinths	15 cm	15 cm
(*Hyacinthus*)	(6 in)	(6 in)
Lilies	18 cm	30 cm
(*Lilium*)	(7 in)	(1 ft)
Snowdrops	7.5 cm	5–8 cm
(*Galanthus*)	(3 in)	(2–3 in)
Squill	7.5 cm	5–8 cm
(*Scilla sibirica*)	(3 in)	(2–3 in)
Tulip	13 cm	10 cm
(*Tulipa*)	(5 in)	(4 in) but wider for bedding

Left: There is still plenty of interest in the herbaceous border with *Crocosmia* (montbretia), *Heliopsis, Helenium* and blue *Salvia splendens* all giving of their best. Deadheading is very important to keep the show going.

Below: *Colchicum speciosum* will be coming into flower. Like the autumn crocus – with which it is often confused – it produces large leaves in spring. Bear this in mind when planting and give it adequate space.

INDOOR BULBS

For growing bulbs in bowls for flowering indoors during the winter, you certainly do not need a greenhouse, but you have to do the right thing at the right time. The earliest to flower are the 'prepared' bulbs, the most popular of which are hyacinths.

They have been treated (not chemically) by the grower so that they will flower much earlier than normal, and they should be planted by the middle of the month in bowls of good quality bulb fibre.

However, because the bowls have to be plunged outdoors for a couple of months, it is often better and safer to start them off in boxes, deep trays or, best of all, in the same bitumenized paper ring culture pots (with the bottoms left in) that are used for tomato growing. These pots are later torn off when you bring the bulbs indoors for transplanting into bowls.

After planting Keep the bulbs as cool as possible for eight to nine weeks. This is best done by plunging them in a bed of moist peat or ground bark in the coolest part of the garden. This treatment is essential if the flower buds are to form properly. If the flowers come out small and highly coloured, it means they weren't kept cool enough, for long enough.

When the tops have grown about 1 in (2·5 cm) usually towards the end of November, bring them into gentle heat indoors. 'Unprepared' bulbs of hyacinths, daffodils, narcissi, and first early tulips can be grown in just the same way, except they need a fortnight or so longer outside and will, in consequence, flower later.

DEADHEADING AND WEEDING

Deadheading will still need to be carried out; roses in particular will benefit from it if they are to continue flowering into the late autumn.

Any hardy annuals that have finished flowering and which are dying should be pulled up and composted.

Keep hoeing so that no late-season weeds run to seed.

PEST CONTROL

The need for pest and disease control should be much reduced by now but you should still keep your eyes open for any late burst of fungus diseases. Roses may still be carrying black spot and, in damp years, grey mould (botrytis) attacks the unopened blooms. Spraying with benomyl will greatly reduce both problems.

HEDGES

If it has been a good growing season, some of the more vigorous hedges might be in need of a final light clipping; really just a tidying up. Never make this severe or you could end up with bare patches through the winter.

PLANTING TREES

This is a good time of year for planting evergreens and conifers. Not only is the ground still warm after the summer, but it is also quite moist. These factors lead to good early root growth and, therefore, quick establishment. Prepare the ground by incorporating well-rotted garden compost, manure or peat, etc, and plant firmly.

Trees and taller shrubs may well need support against autumnal gales. This should take the form of a stake driven in to windward of larger trees and shrubs, but smaller specimens can usually be adequately supported by a stout cane or two.

This is also the month to plant out any trees, shrubs or herbaceous plants that you have been raising from seed.

PROPAGATION

Any hardy annuals that were not sown last month should go in now, or they will be unlikely to make large enough plants to stand a hard winter.

Incidentally, you can still get good results from taking semi-ripe cuttings of hardy shrubs (see **August, flowers and shrubs**). As with seedlings, you should not take them too late or they will be difficult to overwinter, unless they can be kept under cover.

Flag irises Many people lift and divide these lovely tall plants straight after flowering, early in the summer. This is a good system where abundant water can be given to enable them to send out new roots. However, in the drier eastern parts of the country, it is usually wiser to wait until now as rooting and subsequent growth will be more certain.

Lift the clumps, split them up so that only the most recently grown section of rhizome (the flat root, in fact a stem, that sends down the roots) is retained and replanted. To reduce water loss from the rhizome, it is usual to cut the leaves back into a fan shape some 15 cm (6 in) long. Plant firmly, with the top of the rhizome just showing above the soil. *Iris stylosa* can also be planted or divided now.

CONTAINER PLANTS

These will still need close attention to keep them in good condition. Deadhead plants in hanging baskets, tubs and other containers regularly and often to keep them flowering and check every day to see if they need watering. Feeding can usually be reduced to once a fortnight by the end of the month because growth is slowing down. Unless the plants are looking really worn out, they are normally replanted in late October or during November.

LAWNS

There is still plenty of time to sow new lawns if you were unable to do so last month, but try not to delay beyond September since diseases can attack the weak seedlings. Details of sowing a new lawn are given in **August, lawns**. Besides that the stronger a new lawn goes into winter, the better it will be in spring and the sooner you will have a usable lawn.

New lawn care Any lawns that were sown last month or earlier this month can be expected to germinate and start showing green 10–14 days after sowing, provided that the ground has been kept moist. Any stones that appear should be removed without delay.

Once this is done and the new grass has grown to about 2–3 cm (1 in) high, it is time for a light rolling. This will settle the surface so that grass seedlings have a firmer grip on the ground, and it will also level the lawn in preparation for mowing. But note that heavy rolling, especially when the soil is wet, will do more harm than good by causing compaction.

Earthworms are, in the main, the gardener's friends as they aerate the soil. However their casts should be swept off the lawn before they get trodden on.

Another tunnelling creature is the mole. It eats many insect pests which is some comfort when the molehills appear.

Fairy rings may appear as a circle of toadstools or as a broad ring of darker green grass. They should disappear of their own accord.

Weeds Most of those appearing will be annuals and are killed after a few mowings. However, if there are so many that the grass is suffering, the only answer is hand weeding.

The first cut This should be given when the grass is about 6·5 cm (2½ in) long, and the mower blades should be set to at least 2·5 cm (1 in) high, preferably 4 cm (1½ in). This will tidy the lawn and encourage the grass to break out from the base and thicken up. The mowings should then be collected and disposed of because there will almost certainly be a lot of weed seeds amongst them.

Whatever kind of mower you use, it must be really sharp so that the blades of grass are cut and not torn apart. On balance, a rotary mower is better than a cylinder type because, with the latter, a blunt blade can pull the grass seedlings out of the ground.

LAWN PROTECTION
During the early autumn some lawns may attract starlings, which feed on leatherjackets near the surface. Leatherjackets are the grubs of the 'daddy-long-legs' which feed on the roots of the grass. In a dry autumn, they can even kill patches of the grass. If a large number of starlings are gathering on the lawn, it is usually wise to use a lawn pest killer or other soil insecticide as a precaution.

WORMS, MOLES, AND TOADSTOOLS
Worms will also resume their feeding nearer the surface now that the soil is moister. Their casts should be brushed about before mowing.

Moles too will be resuming their activities after the summer and molehills may erupt all over the lawn, see **April, lawns.**

The increased moisture content of the soil in the early autumn often brings on a

Anemone × hybrida is a late-flowering herbaceous perennial with branching stems up to 1 m (3 ft). It grows in sun or light shade.

crop of toadstools. For the most part they are completely harmless to the grass. Water on a general fungicide, such as benomyl or copper, or a specific lawn fungicide, to suppress them if you wish, but they will normally disappear in a couple of weeks anyway.

The exception to the rule is the fungus that causes 'fairy rings'. This is an unsightly rather than damaging disease, and is extremely hard to eradicate.

VEGETABLES
This is a rich month in the garden with many vegetables becoming available, both hard and half-hardy.

VEGETABLES IN SEASON

Continue gathering runner beans, sweet corn, tomatoes, cabbages, cauliflowers, lettuces, marrows and courgettes, cucumbers, beetroot, turnips, carrots, and potatoes. Use them as they become available, and be ready to freeze those that are surplus to your immediate needs.

Outdoor tomatoes   These will be nearing the end of their useful life this month. Even in sunny, warm weather, they are unlikely to produce any more fruits; and the aim should be to ripen those that there are. Ripening can be helped, and hastened, by laying straw on the ground beneath the plants, then cutting the plants away from their supports and laying them on the straw. Erect cloches or polythene tunnels over the plants to protect them for a few weeks more.

Outdoor peppers   Planted outside with other half-hardy vegetables in late May or early June, these can be treated similarly to outdoor tomatoes, but it is usually necessary to fork them slightly out of the ground so that they will lie down without the stem breaking.

CELERY

Certainly the easiest way of growing celery is to select one of the self-blanching varieties such as 'Ivory tower' and 'Golden Self-blanching'. However, whichever variety you choose will necessitate periodic earthing up to help the stems to blanch. When earthing up, do so only to the base of the leafy part of the plant. A final tip – newspaper wrapped around the celery and held in place with string will keep the soil out of the heart of the plant.

EXTRA CONSIDERATIONS

Watering will seldom be necessary this late in the season, but it could still be wanted by recent transplants.

Any remaining sweet peppers should be picked this month.

Sweet corn is another half-hardy vegetable ready for harvesting.

Lettuces   'Dandie' and 'Kwiek' may be sown in frames, as last month, together with New Zealand spinach in the open ground. This is a useful winter vegetable, well worth growing, which makes a nice change from cabbages.

Lettuce seedlings sown last month should be planted in frames or under cloches 23 cm (9 in) apart.

Runner beans   The season will now be drawing to a close, so keep picking the plants regularly to encourage the remainder to develop.

Spring cabbages   Any that were sown last month will be ready for planting in their final positions. With them more than any other brassica, best use can be made of the space by planting them at half the final spacing and use alternate plants early in spring. This will provide a welcome early picking of spring greens. The remaining plants can grow on to maturity. Plant them 23 cm (9 in) apart, in rows 45 cm (18 in) distant.

Apples will be ripening this month. Cordon-trained fruit trees are ideal for the small garden.

APPLE PICKING

September is the beginning of the season for picking apples and pears that are to be stored. Early ripening varieties are best picked selectively so that they are allowed to ripen on the tree. Later varieties, destined for storing, can be picked all at once.

Dessert pears are slightly harder to judge than apples, but they are definitely better if picked when still hard and then ripened indoors. Cooking pears are picked and cooked when still hard. When apples and pears are ready for picking, the former part quite easily from the tree, although pears usually hang on a bit more firmly than apples.

Only completely healthy fruits should be set aside for storing, any showing damage or fungal marks should be put to one side and used first. See the chart for some examples of average picking dates for apples and pears, and the length of time they can be expected to store.

STORAGE

A good storage place must be dark and have a constant and relatively low temperature – 10°C (50°F) is preferable, though hard to find in September. One of the best places is a cellar, but failing that use a good brick outbuilding or garage, preferably with a solid floor. Try to avoid small wooden sheds since the temperature

Pests, diseases and weeds These will be disappearing slowly, provided that you kept on top of them, but they should never be forgotten or ignored. For instance potato blight is still a threat. If it appears, lift and store the potatoes as soon as you can so that the infection does not spread to the tubers.

will also be reaching their peak of cropping. The first three will need picking frequently and regularly so that they are not spoilt by the cooling weather.

For all tree fruits, the greatest danger in the autumn is gales. They will soon knock the fruit to the ground, so always pick as many as you can before a gale is forecast.

FRUIT

The soft fruit season is drawing to a close now. Keep picking the remaining fruits as they become ready. If the weather is changeable, try to gather them dry. Wet fruits are always more likely to attract fungal diseases.

FRUITS IN SEASON

On the other hand the autumn raspberries and perpetual strawberries will now be in full swing. They can be kept going longer by covering the strawberries with cloches or tunnels, and the raspberries with polythene sheeting at night, and during cold or wet days.

Any remaining summer raspberries, blackberries or hybrid cane fruits that have finished fruiting, but still haven't been pruned and trained, should be tackled without delay (see **August, fruit**).

Plums, peaches, figs, apples and pears

PICKING AND STORAGE TIMES FOR APPLES AND PEARS

Variety	Time to pick	Store until
Apples – dessert		
'Blenheim Orange'	Late Sept	Nov–Jan
'Cox's Orange Pippin'	Last week Sept	Nov–Jan
'Egremont Russet'	Late Sept	Oct–Nov
'Greensleeves' (new variety)	Mid Sept	Oct–Nov
'Jupiter' (new variety)	Mid Sept	Oct–Jan
'Laxton's Superb'	Early Oct	Nov–Jan
'Lord Lambourne'	Mid Sept	Sept–Nov
'Spartan' (new variety)	Early Oct	Nov–Feb
'Sturmer Pippin'	Mid Oct	Jan–April
Apples – cooking		
'Annie Elizabeth'	End Sept	Nov–April
'Bramley's Seedling'	Mid Oct	Dec–March
'Lane's Prince Albert'	Late Sept	Dec–March
'Lord Derby'	Late Sept	Oct–Dec
'Newton Wonder'	Mid Oct	Nov–March
Pears		
'Beth'	Sept	Sept
'Onward'	Sept	Late Sept–Early Oct
'Beurre Superfin'	Sept	Sept–Oct
'Conference'	Sept	Oct–Nov
'Doyenne du Comice'	Oct	Nov
'Catillac' (cooking variety)	Oct–Nov	Nov–April

They can also be stored in small batches in polythene bags. Never seal the bags, just fold over the tops.

The best way to store apples is to wrap each fruit individually in newspaper and pack them in boxes.

'Conference' is one of the finest dessert pears. Like other pears it should be stored unwrapped until ripe. All too often pears are eaten when they are still as hard and tasteless as turnips.

changes are great and frequent. Alternatively you could always use a cool, north-facing spare bedroom.

Always remove tins of paint and other strong smelling substances or vegetables, such as onions, from the vicinity of the apples to avoid taint. Exhaust fumes in a garage never do much good either.

Pears keep much better and can be inspected easily if they are laid out in a single layer on shelves, or in boxes.

When apples and pears are brought out of store, remember that it will be 10–14 days before they are ready for eating.

PRUNING

Finish pruning and training fan-trained peaches and nectarines, as described in **August, fruit**. Meanwhile, plum pruning can be carried on from last month.

Trained apple and pear trees which were pruned earlier in the summer, but which had immature shoots left unpruned, can be tackled again to catch those that were previously ignored. Prune them as described in **July, fruit**.

PESTS AND DISEASES

It is normally too late now to take any action against pests and diseases, but a couple of tasks can still be carried out.

The first involves applying a benomyl spray to late apples and pears so that no diseases are stored away with them. The other involves replacing grease bands, which operate on the fly-paper principle, and are fixed around the trunks of fruit trees now for the winter.

Greasebands are designed to catch the wingless female winter and March moths which descend from apple and pear trees at this time of year.

OCTOBER

FLOWERS AND SHRUBS

Given all the raw material that will become available during the next two months or so, a look at the whole process of composting will be useful.

GARDEN COMPOST

This provides the raw material for the important and mysterious humus which encourages growth, and helps plants take in plant food via their roots. Compost also provides a certain amount of plant foods, and thus reduces the need for too many additional fertilizers. It retains moisture and helps make heavy soils workable while putting 'body' into sandy soil.

If you make a compost heap properly, decomposition will start quickly and, in a few days, a good heat will have built up inside. This, in turn, will kill weed seeds, fungal diseases and any pests in the raw material. To make the best compost, the following are required:

● Adequate moisture, but not too much.
● Sufficient air.
● Suitable raw material, preferably a mixture.
● A good activator to start the decomposition process.

Raw material All of the following will help to make excellent garden compost: lawn mowings, most weeds, hedge clippings, spent vegetable plants, flower stalks, leaves of all sorts, soft prunings, sawdust, wood ashes, straw and hay, pet droppings, and animal manures. Also use household waste such as cabbage leaves, vegetable peelings, tea leaves and dead flowers. The only proviso is that they should be vegetative. Fortunately, at this time of year, and into the winter, autumn leaves are plentiful. When composted alone they make leafmould, but it will take about a year to form, even when a suitable activator is used.

Woody hedge clippings, prunings, brassica and herbaceous stalks will normally take a long while to rot down. If shredded first, though, and then composted with an activator and softer materials, they make an invaluable addition to any compost heap. Shredders are available as either hand or electricity operated. The electrical ones are much more effective – they do all the work, are easy to operate and the result is far superior.

Uses There are many uses for garden compost, the main one being for digging into the ground in vegetable plots and flower borders. Roses and shrubs appreciate it especially. Another popular use is as a surface mulch on beds and borders, where it acts as a water retainer and weed smotherer. Also, sifted compost makes a good autumn top-dressing for a lawn. Finally, a sack or porous bag filled with well-rotted compost can be hung in a bucket, or butt of water, to make a weak but very effective liquid feed for plants.

BEGONIAS

Those showy, large-flowered, tuberous-rooted begonias will be dying back soon in the cooler autumn weather. If they were planted in a border, lift the plants carefully, label them with their name and/or description, lay them on their side under cover, keep them dry, and allow them to die right back to the tuber.

Then clean off the dead top and roots and store them in a cold but frost-free place until the spring.

CLEAR SUMMER BEDDING

This month and early November is the time to dig up summer bedding displays

---

PLANTS FOR OCTOBER

Trees and shrubs for autumn colour	Trees and shrubs for fruits and berries		Bulbs
Acer (maples)	Aucuba japonica	Rosa rugosa	Colchicum
Cotinus coggygria	Berberis (barberries)	Sambucus nigra	Crocus (autumn)
Euonymus europaeus (spindle tree)	Cotoneaster	Skimma	Dahlia
Fothergilla major	Crataegus (hawthorn, May)	Sorbus (mountain ash)	Nerine bowdenii
Hamamelis	Euonymus europaeus (spindle tree)	Symphoricarpos (snowberry)	**Herbaceous perennials**
Liriodendron tulipifera	Euonymus latifolia	Viburnum (many)	Anemone japonica (many)
Parrotia persica	Hippophae rhamnoides (sea buckthorn)	**Climbers for autumn colour and fruit**	Helianthus
Prunus	Malus (crab apple)	Clematis orientalis	Kniphofia (red hot poker)
Rhus typhina (stag's horn sumach)	Pyracantha (firethorn)	Clematis tangutica	Liriope muscari
Viburnum carlesii	Rosa moyesii	Parthenocissus quinquefolia (Virginia creeper)	Schizostylis
Viburnum opulus		Vitis (vines)	Sedum
			Solidago (golden rod)

Gladioli corms should be cleaned before storing. Remove the old corm from the base. The cormlets can be grown on to flowering size next year.

Dahlias, certainly in the southern half of the country, will still be in full flower. So, if an early frost threatens, cover them overnight with netting or polythene. This is usually enough to protect them and, with luck, they might keep flowering for another month.

FUCHSIAS

Supposedly half-hardy fuchsias are often a great deal tougher than you would think, especially in the Midlands and south.

Their first winter is the tricky one, so it is a good idea to lift them carefully, cut off all the twiggy growth, dig a deeper hole, replant them and cover their crowns with a good layer of coarse peat, chopped bark or garden compost. If the winter is not excessively severe, the plants stand a very good chance of coming through with flying colours.

Fuchsias growing in pots which you wish to keep them in should be brought inside towards the end of the month, dried off and stored dry (but not parched) in a frost-free but cold building for the winter.

(more raw material for composting), and planting new ones for next spring.

It is always tempting to leave summer displays for as long as possible, but this means that the replacement plants will only have a relatively short time to become established before the winter.

Once the summer display loses its appeal, you should pull it up and replant with a spring display of tulips, hyacinths, wallflowers, and polyanthus.

If you buy your plants choose those that are strong, medium-sized, and healthy; avoid cheap 'end-of-season' offers, they seldom come up to expectations.

Other summer displays of annuals should also be dug up when they have

As with all late-flowering clematis, *C. tangutica* should be cut hard back to about 90 cm (3 ft) in spring.

finished flowering, and the ground either dug in readiness for the next display or left rough for the winter.

GLADIOLI AND DAHLIAS

Any stakes or canes that have been used for supporting gladioli, etc, should be cleaned and dried before being stored away for next year. Look after them as they can be expensive to replace.

Lift gladioli and store them for spring, if this has not already been done (see **September, flowers and shrubs**).

EXTRA CONSIDERATIONS

Start lifting, dividing and replanting any herbaceous plants that have finished flowering and whose foliage is yellowing. Details are given in **November**, the main month for this task.

Continue planting spring flowering bulbs. You ought to have finished by the end of the month, making the best use of the comparatively warm soil.

LAWNS

The mowing season will be drawing to a close now, and the height of cut should be raised by up to 2–3 cm (1 in) to allow the grass to build up strength for the winter.

TURFING

This can begin again after the summer. Up until this point the soil is usually too dry to lift turf successfully, and certainly the weather is often too hot and dry to lay it, unless you have proper facilities for watering the turves in really thoroughly. Otherwise they will turn brown as the roots dry out and probably die.

The ground should be prepared at least one month in advance so that it has time to settle after digging. By now, it should

Left: *Rhus typhina*, stag's horn sumach, is one of the first trees to display brilliant autumn colour. Propagate from suckers which are produced freely.

Below: *Fothergilla major* has fluffy white flowers in spring. It is a small shrub reaching about 1·2 m (6 ft) and needs a lime-free soil.

LAYING TURF

Keep working in this way until the lawn is complete. Brush sifted soil into all the joints and water thoroughly.

Each row is laid half a turf along from the previous row. Lay a plank on the first row and kneel on this while laying the next.

simply be a matter of raking the surface to incorporate a pre-seeding fertilizer, and to create a fine and level tilth. Always buy turf from a reputable source – cheap turf is often thin and full of weeds.

Once the turf has arrived lay it as soon as you can to prevent it from deteriorating. The correct way to lay turf is in the pattern of brickwork (see illustration).

Be sure never to allow it to dry out though, and never use a roller to squash the turves into place. If the turves need that sort of treatment, either they are extremely poor quality or you are doing the job incorrectly.

SCARIFYING
This is raking the lawn as was carried out in March, but now it will get rid of the old dead grass, moss and rubbish that has collected there during the summer. If allowed to remain, this will quickly form a waterproof thatch on top of the soil which will prevent rain from reaching the roots in the summer, and which will also form a wet, soggy winter surface.

In the past, hand-raking was a tiring and tedious job. Now electric scarifiers have made it child's play. The results are also much better.

SPIKING
Spiking is another job that should, if necessary, be done now as well as in March. It will correct any compaction in the surface so that water can drain away

properly and air can circulate right down to the roots. Very seldom is it necessary to spike the whole lawn and, if it is, there is more wrong than compaction.

A garden fork will do a perfectly adequate job in all but really bad cases of compaction, when a hollow-tine spiker is more appropriate. When spiking, aim to

have the rows of holes 10 cm (4 in) apart, and the holes 10 cm (4 in) deep, to the full depth of the fork.

After spiking, the compacted areas will benefit greatly from a top-dressing of sifted soil or soil mixed with fine bark. Apply either at about 1,024 g per m² (2 lb per sq yd) and brush it well into the holes and the sward. This treatment, and a low-nitrogen autumn fertilizer dressing, will strengthen the grass for the winter.

MOSS CONTROL
If moss is a problem, the autumn raking will do a lot to reduce it, but this should be followed by an application of mosskiller (not one mixed with fertilizer and/or weed-killer). A fortnight later, the dead moss will have to be raked out.

Moss is an indication that something is wrong with the lawn and the way it is being looked after. Any number of factors can be responsible for this: drought, poor drainage, starvation, compaction, too close mowing, erratic mowing, and heavy

Collect up leaves with a springbok rake or a besom.

A mechanical leaf sweeper makes easy work of large lawns.

shade are just a few. Any, or all of these factors will have to be remedied if the moss is to be kept away.

LAWN PROBLEMS

Other problems that may arise in a lawn at this time of year are moles, worm casts and the fungal disease Fusarium patch or snow mould. This disease is seen as yellowish dying patches on the lawn which, on closer examination, will be seen to be covered with a fungus.

Overfed lawns are the most susceptible because of their lush growth. Quite good control is had by applying benomyl, but better management, as described above for moss control, is the real answer.

Sweep up the leaves regularly. They are good raw material for the compost heap, or for pure leafmould, if there are enough to make it worthwhile.

VEGETABLES

A general account of composting is given this month in **Flowers and shrubs**, but there is one aspect of it which is more

Pyracantha or firethorn is an evergreen shrub of tremendous value with white flowers in spring and autumn berries. Grow as a wall shrub or as an informal hedge to attract birds into your garden.

relevant to vegetables – what should *not* be put on the compost heap.

The most important category to avoid are the remains of plants which contain soil pests, such as carrot fly and cabbage root fly and soil borne diseases such as club root of brassicas.

Any plants which are known, or thought, to be suffering from any of these ailments should be either burnt or put in the dustbin. If added to the compost heap, there is always the risk that the 'nasties' will survive and attack again next year.

Another potential problem is weeds. Don't forget, they can still set seed.

Cotoneasters also offer a splendid display of berries in autumn. The white flowers, produced in early summer, are attractive to bees. In the foreground the leaves of a *Prunus* turn pink before falling.

CAULIFLOWERS

Although there is little risk of a severe frost this early in the autumn in the Midlands and south, northern gardeners are less fortunate. It is a good idea for them to break off an outside leaf and lay it over any semi-mature or mature curds to keep the frost off.

Most modern varieties have a self-protecting habit, so it is always best to grow them where early frosts are common. The Australian varieties, such as 'Barrier Reef' and 'Brisbane', are especially good in this respect.

LETTUCE AND CABBAGE

A final sowing of lettuce can be made in frames in the first half of the month to give a supply in the spring. Choose a hardy variety, such as 'Valdor' or 'Plus'.

Spring cabbage plants should be planted out in their final positions as soon as possible, if not already done (see **September, vegetables**). If left any later, they may fail to make good plants by the onset of winter. Plant 23 cm (9 in) apart with 45 cm (18 in) between rows.

Left: The season for tree fruit is nearly at an end. Remember that crab apples, as well as being decorative, can be picked to make jelly.

Above: Harvest potatoes carefully. First loosen the soil round the edge of each plant to avoid spearing the tubers. Any that are damaged must be eaten straight away.

POTATOES AND ROOT VEGETABLES

Lift maincrop potatoes by the middle of the month. Dig them up carefully, lay them out to dry, and store them in bags in a cold, dark, frost-free place. An alternative system for storing a large quantity of potatoes and keeping them in good condition is to 'clamp' them (see page 79).

One important point with all root crops is that when lifting them you must be very careful not to stick the fork through them. Any damaged ones should be used up quickly or they will rot.

FRUIT

We are almost at the end of the fruit season now, with the final pickings of apples, pears, perpetual strawberries, late blackberries and autumn-fruiting raspberries.

It is never wise to leave even the latest ripening varieties of apple and pear on the trees after the middle of the month as they face being blown down by gales.

HYGIENE

All fruits which have fallen should be gathered up, no matter why they fell. In many cases, apples, pears and plums drop prematurely because they are harbouring maggots of the codling moth and the red plum maggot. Both will crawl from the fallen fruit, after a few days, and into the ground to pupate.

Fallen leaves These will also be carrying fungal diseases, principally apple and pear scab and mildew, from many fruits. If there is much evidence of this, sweep up the leaves and burn them to prevent infecting new growth next spring. When pruning later on, always be on the lookout for mildewed shoots and canker. Quite good control can be had by cutting them out in winter.

Grease-banding This should be completed without delay as many of the pests the bands are designed to catch will already be leaving the trees (see **September, fruit**).

STRAWBERRIES AND RASPBERRIES

Strawberries can be kept going a bit longer by cloching them or covering them

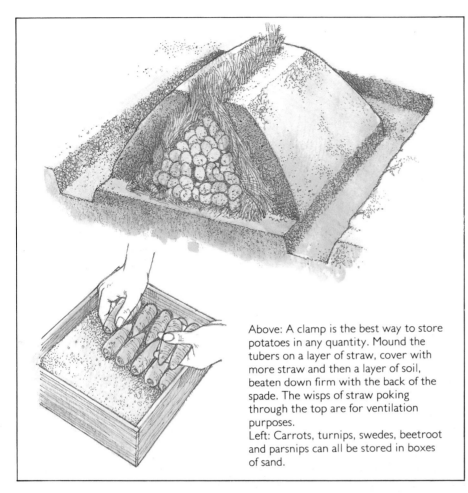

Above: A clamp is the best way to store potatoes in any quantity. Mound the tubers on a layer of straw, cover with more straw and then a layer of soil, beaten down firm with the back of the spade. The wisps of straw poking through the top are for ventilation purposes.

Left: Carrots, turnips, swedes, beetroot and parsnips can all be stored in boxes of sand.

with polythene tunnels. However, remember to ventilate whenever it is warm and/or sunny. Fungal diseases are rife this late in the year and thrive in the close atmosphere under cloches and tunnels.

Finally, autumn raspberries can be protected from the weather with polythene sheeting as and when it is necessary.

PRUNING

Finish pruning blackberries and hybrid cane fruits (loganberry, etc) soon, and tie the new canes in to take the place of the fruited ones cut out previously.

Although blackberries are hardy, some of the hybrids, eg loganberry and tayberry, are not entirely so. It can therefore help to tie all the new canes into a bundle, and fasten this to the wires overwinter. Cut them loose and train in the canes next March, before growth starts.

Start pruning bush fruits when the leaves have begun to fall. This is usually late in October or November, so it is fully dealt with next month.

PREPARATIONS

Decide what new trees, bushes and canes you would like to grow so that they can be bought in good time and planted out before the weather is too cold or wet.

Right: Carrots and beetroots should be lifted and stored at this time of the year as, unlike parsnips, they will spoil if left to stand in cold, wet or frozen ground.

NOVEMBER

FLOWERS AND SHRUBS

Composting should continue with all waste vegetation going onto the heap or into the bin. All the hardy and half-hardy plants that are being pulled up now can be put on the compost heap.

DAHLIAS

Except in the most favoured districts, dahlias will have been killed back by the first really damaging frost of the autumn. When this happens, cut them down to within about 15 cm (6 in) of the ground, label each plant clearly, and dig them out of the ground carefully. Provided that you use it away from the roots, a spade is the best tool for lifting the plants.

Next shake off all the loose soil, turn the tubers upside-down and stand them in trays, or on the floor, in a frost-proof shed or garage to dry. This allows any water to run out of the stems so that it doesn't rot the plants. When the stem is completely dry, like the soil around the roots, gently prize away the soil and snip off any remaining fibrous roots.

You should then dust the tubers with sulphur, or dip them in a dilute solution of benomyl. The latter is more effective but it does mean that the tubers have to be dried again. However, it is effective against storage rots.

Few shrubs are in flower at this time of the year which makes the pink buds and white flowers of *Viburnum tinus* even more welcome. Being evergreen it is ideal at the back of a border or as an informal hedge.

PLANTS FOR NOVEMBER

Deciduous trees and shrubs
See **Plants for October**, as autumn colour and decorative fruits persist into November.

Herbaceous trees and shrubs
Cornus alba 'Elegantissima' and

'Sibirica' (red-stemmed dogwoods)
Cornus stolonifera 'Flaviramea'
Hamamelis virginiana
Rubus cockburnianus
Salix alba 'Chermesina'
Prunus (many have attractive bark)
Prunus subhirtella 'Autumnalis'

Evergreen trees and shrubs
Many conifers and evergreens, especially those with variegated foliage, come into their own this month.
Elaeagnus
Erica × darleyensis
Erica herbacea
Fatsia japonica

Hebe
Viburnum tinus

Climbers
Jasminum nudiflorum

Bulbs
Colchicum
Nerine bowdenii

Herbaceous perennials
Iris stylosa
Liriope muscari

The tubers can now be stored in a dry and frost-free place until the spring. If you are in doubt about the right temperature, the tubers can be stored in boxes of peat or bark, or under a layer of straw. Inspect them occasionally during the winter to check on their condition, and then finally, remember to dry off and store the stakes for another year.

NEW DISPLAYS

Any remaining spring bedding displays must be planted without delay if the plants are to establish themselves and attain a reasonable size before the winter.

If you are interplanting them with bulbs, these too should go in soon although tulips can be planted last of all.

FROST PROTECTION

Any plants still to be protected from frost should be dealt with right away. Quite severe frosts are likely from now on, so half-hardy and tender shrubs could be damaged. Tender shrubs (fuchsias, etc) will most likely be in tubs or pots so they can be brought in under cover for the winter. Climbers trained against walls and fences are best protected by placing straw or bracken over them, and tying this in place with twine for the winter.

As soon as there are signs of growth next spring, remove this protection or the new shoots will develop far too quickly. Half-hardy herbaceous plants can best be protected by heaping crushed bark, coarse peat, straw or bracken over the crowns.

INDOOR BULBS

By the end of the month those bulbs that were planted in bowls or bitumenized paper pots in September (and kept outdoors) for flowering indoors at Christmas, or soon after, should be ready for bringing inside. The timing can be judged by the amount of top growth that they have made (there should be 2–3 cm (1 in) of shoot above the top of the bulb).

Those in paper pots should be transplanted, keeping them intact, into their final ornamental bowls. Bring them indoors into very gentle heat at first, perhaps in an unused or unheated room. If the temperature is much higher, this will result in a lot of leaf and very little flower.

After a couple of weeks when they are growing well, they can be moved into a warmer place.

PRUNING CLIMBERS

Any hardy climbers that have outgrown their position during the summer should be tidied up, cut back and tied in as necessary. This is not a hard pruning, merely an attempt to keep them within bounds and looking tidy. Although this is

All waste vegetation should be composted to enrich the garden in future years. This will include vegetable tops, the remains of ornamental plants and prunings (if shredded). Leaves will form leafmould but should be composted separately as they take longer to break down.

the only pruning people attempt at this time of year, they should also consider tackling smaller specimens.

From now until late March we will be pruning those climbers that flower on the current season's growth. This includes such plants as wisteria, honeysuckle and late flowering clematis.

Wisteria Following the summer pruning (see **July, flowers and shrubs**), the pruned shoots, and any others that have grown since, should be cut back hard to within two buds of their point of origin. This will build up a good flowering spur system on the shrub.

Honeysuckle If necessary, cut out any really old stems that are producing poor quality or few flowers. Tuck in the long, new shoots that will carry next year's flowers and generally tidy up the plant. Finally, never be afraid to cut out large stems – any good honeysuckle will more than make up for this in the following growing season.

Clematis These do not *have* to be pruned as hard as is usually recommended. However, if you do keep them at a manageable size you will produce many large flowers.

If you want to keep your clematis on the more manageable side, cut back all shoots to a fat and healthy bud 30–90 cm (1–3 ft) from the ground. Don't cut them all to the same length or the plant looks unnatural. This treatment will lead to an explosion of growth in the spring, and long flowering in the summer.

PLANNING
Start planning the ornamental side of the garden for next year. This will include any major new tree and shrub plantings, along with bedding schemes, indoor plants that you want to raise yourself, herbaceous plants, etc.

CHRYSANTHEMUMS
Early flowering chrysanthemums should be lifted out of their flowering positions and planted in a cold-frame, or given equally effective protection for the winter. Quite a good system is to plant them in a line in the vegetable garden and cover them with cloches. Alternatively, they can

Easy-going *Elaeagnus pungens* 'Malculata' comes into its own as winter approaches. The dark, glossy green leaves are splashed with patches of golden yellow that add welcome colour at this time of year.

be packed in boxes, their roots covered with moist peat, and kept like this in a shed until the spring.

PLANTING ROSES AND SHRUBS
Start planting bare-rooted and root wrapped roses and shrubs as they become available. This is also a good time to put in container-grown plants. Prepare the sites well because they will be there for a long time and no amount of aftercare will make up for a bad start.

If you are planting a complete border, start by digging it deeply and incorporating plenty of well-rotted compost or manure. The position of each plant should then be marked with a cane so that any alterations can be made before planting.

Each planting hole must then be dug out to a sufficient depth and width to accommodate the rootball or the spread-out root system (if bare rooted or root-wrapped) of each bush. If the plants are bought in containers, the hole should be of a corresponding size with the container being removed before planting.

If just one or two plants are being put in, not a whole border, prepare the site similarly but just dig the immediate area, and work in the compost or manure before digging out the hole. Put the plant in the bottom and replace two or three spadefuls of soil. Give bare-rooted or root-wrapped plants a shake so that the soil falls between the roots, eliminating large air spaces. Next, firmly tread down the soil around the plant and continue filling the hole. If the ground is dry, give it a good watering from a can and finish by tidying up the site and removing footmarks, etc. For the best results, put down a mulch of bark or compost around the new plants. With this sort of thorough preparation

Hippophae rhamnoides, sea buckthorn, makes an ideal windbreak in exposed areas like the seaside.

there is no need to add the time-honoured bonemeal to the soil, though you could sprinkle a general fertilizer around the plants in spring.

Finally, beware of slugs and snails. Slug pellets give the best protection, but, if you have qualms about their safety, put them under a tile or slate so that only the intended victims can reach them.

ROSES

If you grow roses, the main job this month is tidying them up for the winter. Note, however, that this does not involve heavy pruning, which is carried out, and described, in **March, flowers and shrubs**. Ramblers will have been attended to in July, after flowering.

Climbers should have all their dead heads removed, while their long shoots (irrespective of whether you intend keeping them) must be tied in to stop them being blown about and damaged.

Hybrid tea and floribunda bushes

should also be given a final deadheading. At the same time, remove all developing flower buds to ensure that the plants are forced to start their annual winter rest, without which they would soon become worn out.

Any long shoots must also be shortened back so that there is nothing which will be lashed about in the winter winds. Not only will the shoots suffer damage, but they will also cause the bush to rock about, leading to a puddle around the base of the stem which often leads to collar rot and the death of the bush. Finally, firmly tread in all plants.

DECIDUOUS SHRUBS

This can also be the start of the pruning season for many deciduous shrubs (those that lose their leaves). They include late-flowering ceanothus and hypericum, plants which have flowered since June on this season's shoots. In cold districts, pruning is best left until March to take

DIVIDING HERBACEOUS PERENNIALS

Two digging forks are driven in the centre, back to back, and levered together. Discard the woody centre and replant the younger, outer pieces.

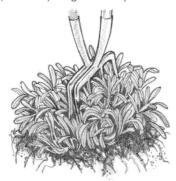

Small clumps can usually be teased apart with the fingers or a handfork. Large clumps will need tougher treatment.

Cut irises, lupins and red hot pokers into portions with an old knife. Again, only replant the young vigorous pieces.

account of any frost damage during the winter. No formal pruning is usually needed, the aim being to keep the shrubs of a manageable size, tidy and open. Any shoots or branches which are growing out of place should therefore be removed, together with any broken or damaged wood, and branches causing overcrowding within the shrub.

If the plant is becoming leggy with all the new growth at the top, the base being mainly woody and without flowers, one or two of the older branches can be cut back to encourage new growth.

HERBACEOUS PLANTS

Herbaceous plants should be tidied up for the winter now by cutting down to the ground those whose leaves are dying down and going yellow.

Dividing Splitting and replanting should be tackled at this time every three years or so to prevent the middle of the clumps becoming old and worn out (see illustration). If there is a large amount of splitting up to do, work along the border systematically, making sure that you keep each variety separate and labelled. If they end up in small, unmarked heaps all over the lawn, the term 'mixed border' will take on a completely, new meaning!

Replanting the border Once all the plants have been lifted, dig over the border, working in plenty of garden compost or manure. Then, lay out all the material

you are going to replant, together with any new purchases. This will give you a good chance to juggle them about, finding the best places and spacings so that you end up with exactly what you want.

The planting distances are obviously governed by the height and spread of the individual plants, but 30–45 cm (12–18 in) between varieties is a good average spacing. Always plant firmly so that the crown of the plant is just below the surface because the soil is going to settle down; if you plant them at the right depth now they'll end up high and dry by the spring.

Also, occasionally check during the winter whether any have been lifted by the frost. If so, tread them down.

HARDWOOD CUTTINGS

November is a good time for taking hardwood (mature) cuttings of many shrubs, especially deciduous ones.

Use only strong and disease-free shoots of this season's growth; those on the sunny side of the shrub are likely to be the best. Remove the shoot, trim back the base so that it ends with a bud, and cut off the top to leave 10–15 cm (4–6 in). If the removed top is large enough, another cutting can be taken from it. All cuttings should end with a bud, top and bottom.

A V slit is made in the ground with a spade and the cuttings inserted into the slit 5–8 cm (2–3 in) apart so that about half their length is buried. The soil is then firmed around them with the feet.

It is seldom necessary to treat the base

of these cuttings with a rooting hormone, but it will do no harm. The base of each cutting should heal over during the winter, and roots start to appear in the spring.

LAWNS

If the full autumn maintenance treatment was not given last month, it should be undertaken soon so that any disturbances will have time to put themselves right before the winter. In a few weeks the grass will have stopped growing and improvements will be delayed until the spring – this can be a long time to wait if scarification was rather harsh on the sward. Full details of the treatment were given in **October, lawns.**

By the end of November the lawn should hardly have to be cut at all. Any mowing should be set to at least 4 cm (1½ in) so that the grass is just topped, not really mowed. Keep brushing off any leaves, and add them to the compost heap.

VEGETABLES

Keep using fresh vegetables as they become ready, along with stored ones.

Vegetables in season Fresh vegetables may include Brussels sprouts, cabbages, cauliflowers, lettuces in frames, celery, leeks, and parsnips. Stored vegetables may consist of the following: carrots, onions and shallots, potatoes, turnips, swedes, and beetroot.

November sees the end of half-hardy vegetables, such as runner beans, sweet corn, marrows, courgettes and outdoor tomatoes and cucumbers. As they become spent, pull them up and set them aside for composting, remembering to exclude any that have pests and diseases.

COMPOSTING

This is the real end of the gardening season, and is the time when it is traditional to turn out the compost heap in readiness for digging it into the vegetable plot this month. Lots of material will become available for the compost heap once the first damaging frost strikes.

CLEARING THE GROUND

With the end of the summer and early autumn vegetables, much of the vegetable patch will be ready for digging. If your garden is on heavy clay, try to get this deep digging done as early as you can in the winter so that the weather has the maximum amount of time in which to break down the soil before the spring activity. Leave the ground as rough as you can so that the greatest surface area is exposed to the weather.

Light, sandy land is best left until the spring before it is dug. This will help it to retain all the available moisture.

Digging A spade is the normal tool used for digging but, on heavy land, a good fork is much easier and will do the job just as well, provided that the soil holds together. The right way to dig is to hold the spade or fork as near upright as is comfortable, so that it can be driven in to its full depth. It also makes sure that any compost or weeds you want to bury are deep under ground.

Digging to one spade's depth is called **single digging**, but for gardens that have either been neglected or which are brand new, a more effective way of bringing the soil into working order is **double digging**. While the principle is the same, the trench that is formed in single digging is then itself dug with a fork to a further 25–30 cm (10–12 in) deep (see illustrations). When a reasonably large plot has to be dug, it helps to divide it in two, and tackle one half at a time. Once digging is complete, avoid walking on the dug land until you cultivate it in the spring.

SOWING

'Aquadulce' broad beans, or any others listed as suitable for autumn sowing, may be sown early in the month. Allow 45 cm (18 in) between rows, with 12 cm (4–5 in) between seeds. They will withstand the winter as young plants, and will give you a feed of beans two to three weeks ahead of those sown next spring. They are also said to be less susceptible to attack from black-fly, but this tends to vary with the season and certainly does not mean that they can be disregarded.

FROST PROTECTION

If cauliflowers and celery have not been protected from frost and still need covering, protect the celery with straw or bracken, and cauliflowers by breaking off an outside leaf and placing it over the curd.

Brussels sprouts and purple sprouting broccoli plants will need supporting in all

---

DOUBLE DIGGING

First dig out a strip of top soil to one spade's depth and pile to one side.

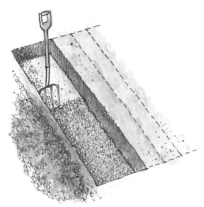

Fork over the subsoil and, at the same time, incorporate a generous amount of well rotted manure or garden compost.

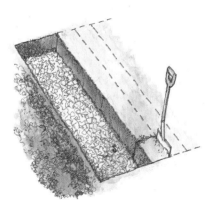

The next strip of top soil is thrown forwards onto the improved subsoil.

Continue in this way, working systematically along the bed or border – see illustration on page 86.

DIGGING A PLOT

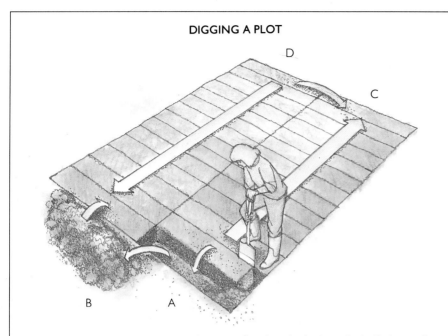

Divide the plot into two. Dig out a trench at A and pile up the soil at B. The next trip of soil is turned over and forwards (as described on page 85).

Continue back along the half-plot until trench C. Fill this with soil from trench D. Carry on digging the second half-plot until you reach the final trench which can be filled with soil B.

but the most sheltered gardens. The best method is to drive a thin stake or stout cane into the ground beside them, before tying the plants to it. Added support will be given if the cane tops are joined firmly together with a length of strong twine passing along the row.

Finally, all fallen brassica leaves and other vegetable debris should be collected regularly and composted.

FRUIT

Tidy up the plants of perpetual strawberries by removing any dead leaves and spent fruit stalks. Do not cut them back in the same way as you would summer varieties (see **July, fruit**).

PRUNING RED CURRANTS AND GOOSEBERRIES

These can be pruned now and are treated in the same way as bushes growing on a short trunk (leg). They are made up of semi-permanent branches, which are only cut out when the quality and quantity of their fruit deteriorates.

Many gardeners claim the flavour of parsnips is improved by the first frost. However, frosted ground will also mean that the roots cannot be lifted until a thaw. It is as well to lift a few early and store them in sand (see page 79).

digging up and planting in their final position one year later.

Black currants Grown as stools, these have many shoots originating at and below ground level. The cuttings are of the same length as for red currants, but instead no buds are removed, and the cuttings are inserted so that only the top three or four are showing. This results in many of the underground buds sending out shoots as well as roots. As before, the cuttings can be lifted after one year. No hormone rooting powder is needed for any of these hardwood cuttings.

EXTRA CONSIDERATIONS
Check on the condition of fruit cages and renew or mend any damaged side netting. In rural areas where gooseberries are grown in a cage, the top should be kept on to prevent bird damage. Otherwise, the top netting should be taken off to allow in birds to clear up any insect pests.

Finish pruning and tying in cane fruits (except autumn raspberries).

Pests and diseases Peach and almond trees infected with peach leaf curl should be sprayed with a copper spray as soon as the leaves have fallen. This is in addition to the February spray.

In rural areas, make sure that bullfinches and tits are not pecking out and eating the buds, particularly of gooseberries and plums. At the first sign of damage, treat with a harmless chemical deterrent, based on aluminium ammonium sulphate. If the trees are still small, put netting over them.

Planting Newly arrived tree, bush and cane fruits should be planted in their permanent positions or, if this is not possible, heeled in until it is.

Apples and pears Pick and store any remaining fruits before they are blown down or otherwise damaged.

Check any stored apples and pears and remove any that are showing signs of deteriorating or ripening.

Apples and pears that were summer pruned should be looked at and, if there has been any growth from the pruned shoots, this should be cut back to the point of origin.

Basic pruning consists of keeping the bushes open by removing crossing, crowded, and out-of-place branches. However, for the best results, a slightly more sophisticated system is called for, so that maximum crops of high quality berries are produced. For this, all new shoots are cut back to two buds in the winter, whether summer pruned (see **June, vegetables**) or not, so that a fruiting spur system is created on the branches.

BLACK CURRANTS
These produce their best fruit on shoots younger than about four years old.

Pruning therefore consists mainly of cutting out to the ground branches that are four and more years old, to make room for younger ones. Along with these must go branches that are too low, or otherwise clearly out of place, and those which are causing overcrowding. Diseased and broken branches must be removed.

Break off an outer leaf to cover a cauliflower curd. This will keep it white and protect it from frost. Self-protecting varieties are available with inner leaves that enclose the curd.

PROPAGATION
Gooseberries and all types of currants can be propagated very easily from hardwood (mature) cuttings. Cut off strong, straight and healthy shoots of this year's growth. The top and bottom of each shoot is cut back to a bud so that the resulting cuttings are about 25 cm (10 in) long.

Red currants and gooseberries These should be on a leg, all buds except the top three or four are nicked out. A V-slit is then made in the ground with a spade, and the cuttings are pushed into a 15 cm (6 in) or so apart, so that the lowest retained bud is about 13 cm (5 in) above the ground. The cuttings will be ready for

DECEMBER

FLOWERS AND SHRUBS

The herbaceous border and other perennials around the garden will be looking a sorry sight by now and, unless there are some late ones still in flower, they should be cut down to the ground and put on the compost heap. Clean and put away for the winter any supporting canes, etc.

PROTECTION

One herbaceous plant which will shortly be coming into flower is the Christmas rose (*Helleborus niger*). The main problem with this rightly popular flower is its susceptibility to weather damage. To protect the buds and flowers from this, put a cloche over the clumps or just a sheet of glass resting on bricks or large stones. Either will give them enough shelter. Some alpine plants and several of the choicer winter flowering crocuses will also benefit from this action.

SWEET PEAS AND WALLFLOWERS

This is a good time to prepare a sweet pea trench. Although a new one can be dug and lined with garden compost, you can often save yourself work by using last summer's runner bean trench, revitalizing it with additional and fresh compost.

Once wallflower plants have settled in and are showing signs of growing away,

the tops should be pinched out to encourage a bushy appearance and also to restrict the height.

TREES, SHRUBS AND ROSES

Container-grown and root-wrapped or bare-rooted specimens can all be planted now, provided that the soil and weather are in good shape (see **November, flowers and shrubs**).

All tree stakes should be looked at critically and replaced if necessary. Most trees will be self-supporting after three or four years, and there is seldom any point in having a stake beyond that time. If the tree is holding up the stake, quite clearly there is no need for it. Ties should also be examined and slackened off if at all tight.

You will have finished using a lot of what might be called 'summer tools' now (hoes, rakes, etc). They should be cleaned thoroughly, oiled lightly, and hung up for the winter where they will stay dry.

LAWNS

If you are planning to put down a new lawn from seed in the spring, start deep digging whenever the soil is in a workable condition so that it has time to settle down before sowing. The more you can walk on it, levelling and raking, between now and sowing, the better.

PROTECT CHRISTMAS ROSE

Protect the flowers from damp and cold with a sheet of glass.

During the winter, check the lawn after heavy rain to see if there are any low spots where the rain forms puddles. If there are any wait until they dry out, and then spike the areas to correct possible compaction. If this fails to cure the problem, it probably means that the ground needs raising.

EXTRA CONSIDERATIONS

If wormcasts are troublesome on lawns, brush them off when they are dry. Avoid walking on a lawn when it is covered in frost. Your feet will crush the frozen grass and will leave dark green patches on the surface. Finally, brush off leaves regularly and add them to the compost heap.

PLANTS FOR DECEMBER

Deciduous trees and shrubs

Cornus alba 'Elegantissima' and 'Sibirica' (red-stemmed dogwoods)
Cornus stolonifera 'Flaviramea'
Cotoneaster
Daphne mezereum
Hamamelis (witch hazel)

Lonicera fragrantissima
Prunus subhirtella 'Autumnalis'
Rubus cockburnianus
Salix alba 'Chermesina'
Viburnum × bodnantense

Evergreen trees and shrubs

Aucuba japonica
Erica herbacea (many cultivars)

Enonymus japonicus 'Ovatus Aureus'
Fatsia japonica
Hippophae rhamnoides (sea buckthorn)
Ilex (holly)
Mahonia
Pyracantha (firethorn)
Sorbus
Taxus (yew)
Viburnum tinus

Climbers
Jasminum nudiflorum

Bulbs
Crocus
Cyclamen coum
Galanthus (snowdrop)

Herbaceous perennials
Helleborus niger
Iris stylosa
Winter-flowering pansies

Above: *Ilex aquifolium* 'Golden King' is a fine holly for any garden with its variegated foliage and berries.

Right: *Helleborus niger*, the Christmas rose, needs a shady position and moist soil. Divide with care in spring.

Iris stylosa
(I. unguicularis)
flowers throughout
the winter. Plant in
a sunny position, in
well drained soil. It
spreads by rhizomes
(underground
stems) and large
clumps can be split
up in September.

VEGETABLES

Celery is a far from hardy crop and will need to be protected with straw or bracken once the winter really sets in. If you are in a windy site, put netting or soil on the straw to keep it in place.

Although parsnips and leeks are perfectly hardy, in the depths of winter the ground is frequently frozen hard. This makes it very difficult to dig them out without damaging them. To prevent this, lay straw or bracken amongst them to stop the ground being frozen too deeply.

Look at stored vegetables occasionally to make sure that all is well. Onions, potatoes (keep them frost-free), parsnips, carrots, turnips and swedes all store well but, if any diseased ones are found, remove them immediately as the infection will spread to others.

Although Christmas is nearly upon us, it is time to think about what you want to grow in the coming year. Try to buy seeds as soon as you can so that you get exactly what you want and are not disappointed.

DOUBLE DIGGING

In November, you started digging the vacant plots where vegetables had been. If you have just moved into a new house, or if the crops in your existing garden are not what they should be, it may well be that the ground needs double digging. The operation is explained in **November, vegetables** and can still be carried out in December provided the soil is in a fit state.

PESTS

The main pest at this time of year in country areas is likely to be pigeons. They will quickly strip brassica plants if allowed to. Protecting the plants with netting, or even growing brassicas in a fruit cage, are the only effective ways of keeping them off. In a really hard winter, few green vegetables are safe. Even in towns feral pigeons can be a nuisance.

FRUIT

If you grow fruit, an important job in late December and January is winter washing (spraying) the trees and bushes with tar oil to kill the overwintering stages of many of the worst pests, including greenfly eggs. It is a messy job, so you will need to wear very old clothes and rubber

Savoy cabbage is one of the vegetables available for picking now.

Others include Brussels sprouts, cauliflowers, celery, leeks and parsnips.

gloves. This should only be done after pruning has been finished. Also, because of the scorching effect that tar oil has on foliage, it should only be done when the trees and bushes are completely leafless and dormant, ie in December, January, and the first half of February.

For the same reason, if there are any plants (vegetables, ornamentals or lawns) beneath the trees being sprayed, they should be covered with newspaper during the actual spraying.

You should avoid winter washing when the temperature is below freezing. Apply the spray so that it really gets under the bark, penetrates into all the little nooks and crannies and runs down the branches and trunk. Remember that most of the pests will be completely hidden.

PLANTING

When bare-rooted or root-wrapped trees and bushes are purchased, they should be dealt with in one of three ways:

● Plant them straight away in their permanent positions.

● Heel them in temporarily until you are ready, or until conditions are right for them to be planted properly.

● Keep them wrapped up and put them under cover. This is usually only necessary when the weather is too bad even to heel them in.

PROTECTION

Although most fruit trees and bushes are quite hardy, vines, kiwi fruit and hybrid cane fruits (loganberries in particular) are amongst those that may suffer in prolonged cold spells unless bundled together. If necessary, protect them with sacking or netting during the worst of the weather. Make sure that this covering will stay in place during rough weather.

TREE AND BUSH TIES

All stakes and ties should be checked to see that they are in working order and not causing any problems to the trees, such as rubbing or constricting growth. This applies to trees and bushes trained to wires and/or canes, just as much as to those in the open garden.

PRUNING

Another major task now is pruning. Although there are, of course, different ways of pruning each kind of fruit and, indeed, the same kind of fruit, it is a much simpler job to tackle than many newcomers to gardening think.

APPLES AND PEARS

The two most common methods of pruning 'bush' apple and pear trees (those with a short trunk) are by the regulated and renewal systems.

The regulated system This is like an annual winter service. It involves the removal of only those branches and shoots which, for one reason or another, need to go. This includes overcrowded, dead, diseased or broken branches, one shading another, and any that are too high, too low, or crossing from one side of the tree to the other. In fact, any branch which is

damaged or out of place, or which is preventing others from growing and fruiting properly.

This certainly improves the appearance and general well-being of the tree, but it is only of limited benefit as regards an improvement in the quantity and quality of the crops.

The renewal system On the other hand, this is designed to do all that the regulated does, while keeping the tree young by 'renewing' old branches so that it crops well and heavily. The previous rules still apply, but they should be carried out with a view to making sure that the tree is furnished with plenty of young slender fruit-bearing wood.

Any branch that has to go should be cut back to a younger one nearer its point of origin. Similarly, if two branches are competing for space, preference is normally given to the younger. Thus every main branch will have younger replacement branches being built up on it to take over when the need arises.

Prunings make an excellent ingredient for the compost. They help to keep the heap open and the wood gives rise to more humus than anything else. They do have to be shredded before composting or they will take too long to break down.

DISEASE

Mention has been made of cutting out diseased branches. On apple trees, the most likely cause of this will be the disease canker. This fungus eats into the bark and wood and will, if it goes completely round a branch, kill it. If, when pruning, you notice that a tree bears any of these canker lesions, look at them closely and, if they encircle a branch, saw it off and paint the wound. If the lesion does not go all round, cut it out with a sharp knife and paint over the scar with a fungicidal paint.

Finally, relax and have a happy Christmas ready for the new gardening year!

INDEX

ACKNOWLEDGEMENTS

The publishers wish to thank the following photographers and organizations for their kind permission to reproduce the following photographs in this book:
Eric Crichton 12, 15, 19, 20t, 21, 22b, 24b, 28b, 30tl, 30tr, 49t, 54r, 67b, 71, 77tl, 80, 83, 89b; The Garden Picture Library/Perdereau-Thomas 9, 13b, 22tl, 78,/Brian Carter 11, 13t, 46,/David Russel 36; The Harry Smith Collection 25t & b. The following photographs were specially taken for the Octopus Publishing Group Picture Library:
Michael Boys 55r, 63r, 75, 79, 87; W F Davidson 10, 20b, 35, 62, 66l; Jerry Harpur 6, 7, 24t, 29, 31r, 33b, 41, 43l, 44, 47r, 49b, 53t, 54l, 59, 72, 78, 90, 92; Neil Holmes 37, 56, 82, 86; George Wright 16, 18, 23, 38, 53, 69, 70, 77tr, 91; Octopus 8, 14, 17, 22tr, 26, 27, 28t, 31l, 33t, 34, 42, 43r, 45, 47l, 48, 51b, 52, 55l, 57, 60tl, 61, 63l, 64, 67t, 68, 74, 75b, 76, 81, 89t, 93.

Illustrations by Jim Robins.